Biography Today

*Profiles
of People
of Interest
to Young
Readers*

Volume 16
Issue 3
September 2007

Cherie D. Abbey
Managing Editor

*P.O. Box 31-1640
Detroit, MI 48231-1640*

Cherie D. Abbey, *Managing Editor*

Joan Axelrod-Contrada, Laurie DiMauro, Joan Goldsworthy,
Laurie Hillstrom, Justin Karr, Leslie Karr, and Tom Wiloch, *Sketch Writers*

Allison A. Beckett and Mary Butler, *Research Staff*

* * *

Peter E. Ruffner, *Publisher*
Matthew P. Barbour, *Senior Vice President*
Kay Gill, *Vice President—Directories*

* * *

Elizabeth Collins, *Research and Permissions Coordinator*
Kevin Hayes, *Operations Manager*
Cherry Stockdale, *Permissions Assistant*

Shirley Amore, Martha Johns, and Kirk Kauffman, *Administrative Staff*

The information in this publication was compiled from the sources cited and from other sources considered reliable. While every possible effort has been made to ensure reliability, the publisher will not assume liability for damages caused by inaccuracies in the data, and makes no warranty, express or implied, on the accuracy of the information contained herein.

This book is printed on acid-free paper meeting the ANSI Z39.48 Standard. The infinity symbol that appears above indicates that the paper in this book meets that standard.

Printed in the United States

INDEXED IN
Children's Magazine Guide

Contents

Preface

Biography Today is a magazine designed and written for the young reader—ages 9 and above—and covers individuals that librarians and teachers tell us that young people want to know about most: entertainers, athletes, writers, illustrators, cartoonists, and political leaders.

The Plan of the Work

The publication was especially created to appeal to young readers in a format they can enjoy reading and readily understand. Each issue contains approximately 10 sketches arranged alphabetically. Each entry provides at least one picture of the individual profiled, and bold-faced rubrics lead the reader to information on birth, youth, early memories, education, first jobs, marriage and family, career highlights, memorable experiences, hobbies, and honors and awards. Each of the entries ends with a list of easily accessible sources designed to lead the student to further reading on the individual and a current address. Retrospective entries are also included, written to provide a perspective on the individual's entire career.

Biographies are prepared by Omnigraphics editors after extensive research, utilizing the most current materials available. Those sources that are generally available to students appear in the list of further reading at the end of the sketch.

Indexes

Cumulative indexes are an important component of *Biography Today*. Each issue of the *Biography Today* General Series includes a Cumulative Names Index, which comprises all individuals profiled in *Biography Today* since the series began in 1992. In addition, we compile three other indexes: the Cumulative General Index, Places of Birth Index, and Birthday Index. See our web site, www.biographytoday.com, for these three indexes, along with the Names Index. All *Biography Today* indexes are cumulative, including all individuals profiled in both the General Series and the Subject Series.

Our Advisors

This series was reviewed by an Advisory Board comprised of librarians, children's literature specialists, and reading instructors to ensure that the concept of this publication—to provide a readable and accessible biographical magazine for young readers—was on target. They evaluated the title as it developed, and their suggestions have proved invaluable. Any errors, however, are ours alone. We'd like to list the Advisory Board members, and to thank them for their efforts.

Gail Beaver
Adjunct Lecturer
University of Michigan
Ann Arbor, MI

Cindy Cares
Youth Services Librarian
Southfield Public Library
Southfield, MI

Carol A. Doll
School of Information Science and Policy
University of Albany, SUNY
Albany, NY

Kathleen Hayes-Parvin
Language Arts Teacher
Birney Middle School
Southfield, MI

Karen Imarisio
Assistant Head of Adult Services
Bloomfield Twp. Public Library
Bloomfield Hills, MI

Rosemary Orlando
Director
St. Clair Shores Public Library
St. Clair Shores, MI

Our Advisory Board stressed to us that we should not shy away from controversial or unconventional people in our profiles, and we have tried to follow their advice. The Advisory Board also mentioned that the sketches might be useful in reluctant reader and adult literacy programs, and we would value any comments librarians might have about the suitability of our magazine for those purposes.

Your Comments Are Welcome

Our goal is to be accurate and up-to-date, to give young readers information they can learn from and enjoy. Now we want to know what you think. Take a look at this issue of *Biography Today*, on approval. Write or call me with your comments. We want to provide an excellent source of biographical information for young people. Let us know how you think we're doing.

Cherie Abbey
Managing Editor, *Biography Today*
Omnigraphics, Inc.
P.O. Box 31-1640
Detroit, MI 48231-1640

editor@biographytoday.com
www.biographytoday.com

Congratulations!

Congratulations to the following individuals and libraries, who are receiving a free copy of *Biography Today,* Vol. 16, No. 3, for suggesting people who appear in this issue:

Carol Arnold, Hoopeston Public Library, Hoopeston, IL

Dorey Brown, Troy Middle School, Troy, MO

Anna Flora, Knox Middle School, Knox, IN

Mitchell Robey, Norton, MA

Lisa Scharf, Ridge Junior High School, Mentor, OH

Carmelo Anthony 1984-

American Professional Basketball Player with the Denver Nuggets
Second-Leading Scorer in the NBA for the 2006-07 Season

BIRTH

Carmelo Kyan Anthony—known by the nickname "Melo"—was born on May 29, 1984, in Brooklyn, a section of New York City. When he was two years old, his Puerto Rican father, Carmelo Iriarte, died of liver failure. From this time on, Carmelo was raised primarily by his African-American mother, Mary Anthony, who worked as a housekeeper. He had two older brothers, Robert and Wilford, an older sister, Michelle, and an older half-sister, Daphne. Since all of Carmelo's siblings were more than ten years older than him, he spent much of his youth as the only child at home.

YOUTH

When Carmelo was eight years old, his mother took a job in housekeeping at the University of Baltimore. They two of them moved to Baltimore, Maryland. They lived in a townhouse on the west side of the city, in a gritty neighborhood known as "The Pharmacy" for its large number of drug dealers.

> "Everything in my household had God in it," Anthony recalled. "Posters with inscriptions. Two or three Bibles in every room. That was the meaning of God to me. Now that I'm older, I recognize that God is everywhere."

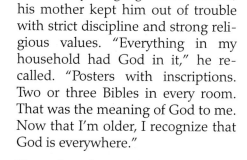

Although young Carmelo was surrounded by drugs, guns, and crime, his mother kept him out of trouble with strict discipline and strong religious values. "Everything in my household had God in it," he recalled. "Posters with inscriptions. Two or three Bibles in every room. That was the meaning of God to me. Now that I'm older, I recognize that God is everywhere."

Throughout his youth, Carmelo spent most of his spare time playing basketball. He played in the streets with neighborhood friends, at a local recreation center, and on various school teams. In fact, his mother's most effective method of discipline was to revoke his court privileges. By the time he reached high school, he had gained a reputation as one of the most talented young players in Baltimore.

EDUCATION

Anthony attended Towson Catholic High School. It was located on the other side of Baltimore from his neighborhood, so he traveled 45 minutes each way by bus and train to get to school every day. Given his natural basketball talent and growing local reputation, he had no trouble making the varsity team at Towson as a freshman. But staying on the team turned out to be a bigger challenge for him.

Anthony did not bother to work hard on the court or in the classroom. Because of his laziness, bad attitude, and poor grades, he was being dropped

Anthony with his mother, Mary Anthony.

from the varsity team. "As a good player in the inner city, you're always hearing people say you're better than you really are and that you don't have to do things like everybody else," he explained. "When I was in Baltimore I took all that talk and ran with it. It distracted me from my schoolwork. I started getting suspended."

Fortunately, losing his spot on the team made an impact on Anthony. He started taking both school and basketball more seriously, and he dedicated himself to working hard and improving. During his junior season, his skills attracted the attention of Jim Boeheim, coach of the Syracuse University Orangemen. Boeheim offered the young player a scholarship, and Anthony committed to Syracuse.

Over the summer between his junior and senior years, Anthony performed well in a number of summer camps and tournaments against other talented players. He suddenly went from being considered a solid regional recruit to one of the top high-school basketball players in the country. In fact, some analysts indicated that he might be good enough to skip college and play professionally straight out of high school. "I was reading my name on the Internet. People were writing about me going to the NBA," he recalled. "I wasn't even thinking about it at first. Then I did. It's hard not to think about it."

If he did want to play college basketball, Anthony knew that he needed to improve his grades and earn a qualifying score on a standardized college aptitude test like the ACT. He took the ACT exam several times, but he always came up a few points short of the required score. "Without the score I'd have no choice," he acknowledged. "I would have gone to the NBA."

Transferring to a National Powerhouse

For his senior year in high school, Anthony hoped to improve his academic performance and showcase his basketball talents. So he decided to transfer to Oak Hill Academy, a Baptist boarding school in rural Virginia. Oak Hill traditionally boasts one of the best high-school basketball teams in the country and has produced several NBA players over the years. The academy also emphasizes strict discipline and high academic standards. All students are required to wear uniforms, stay on campus, and observe a bedtime.

Before Anthony was accepted to Oak Hill, he had to complete five weeks of summer school in order to catch up academically. "He would go to classes from 7 A.M. to noon, six days a week, and then at 2 P.M. each day he had to meet me at the gym," recalled Coach Steve Smith. "It would be 100 degrees, with no air-conditioning, and we would work him out for two hours, all by himself. Then he would have study hall."

Anthony's hard work in the gym paid off in a terrific senior year. Averaging 21.7 points and 7.4 rebounds per game, he led Oak Hill to a 32-1 record and a number three national ranking. The highlight of the season came in February 2002, when Anthony scored 34 points in a victory over St. Vincent-St. Mary of Akron, Ohio, a top prep team. The team was led by junior standout LeBron James, who went on to star for the NBA's Cleveland Cavaliers. (For more information on James, see *Biography Today Sports*, Vol. 12.) In recognition of his great season, Anthony was named a first-team high-school All-American.

Anthony's hard work in the classroom paid off as well. After several more attempts, he managed to earn a high enough score on the ACT to enable him to go to college. No one was more thrilled about this achievement than his mother. "I didn't want him to go to the NBA," Mary Anthony admitted. "When you get all that fame and fortune, honey, you become a man, right then and there. I wanted my son to have a chance to be 18 years old." Anthony graduated from Oak Hill in 2002 and enrolled as a freshman at Syracuse University. Ultimately, he spent only one year at Syracuse before leaving college to join the NBA.

Dunking for the Syracuse University Orangemen.

CAREER HIGHLIGHTS

College—The Syracuse University Orangemen

At Syracuse, Anthony became a star from the moment he walked onto the basketball court. He scored 27 points and grabbed 11 rebounds in his first college game, then went on to start every game of the 2002-03 NCAA season at small forward. Anthony led the Orangemen in points per game, with 22.2, and in rebounds, with 10.0. His strong performance helped Syracuse post a 30-5 record for the year.

With Anthony's help, the Orangemen earned a spot in the NCAA tournament. This prestigious event features the top 64 teams in college basketball. They play a single-elimination tournament to decide the national championship. Most analysts thought that Syracuse was too young and inexperienced to advance far in the tournament. But Anthony showed great maturity and helped keep his teammates focused. The team surprised many observers by advancing through the first four rounds to reach the Final Four.

Syracuse faced the University of Texas in its Final Four matchup, and Anthony turned in his best performance of the entire year. He scored a season-high 33 points and added 14 rebounds to lead his team to a 95-84 victory and a spot in the title game. A few days later, Anthony contributed 20 points, 10 rebounds, and 7 assists to help the Orangemen defeat the University of Kansas Jayhawks by a score of 81-78. Syracuse claimed its first NCAA national basketball championship, and Anthony was named Final Four most valuable player. "When I first cut the net down, I thought it was the greatest thing that ever happened to me," he remembered. "But it didn't sink in right away. It took me two or three months to realize that I actually won a national championship."

Despite his outstanding season and spectacular tournament performance, Anthony did not win many individual awards following his freshman year. Some voters snubbed him because they believed he would only play one year for Syracuse before jumping to the NBA. They preferred to reward upperclassmen who had paid their dues in college basketball. But Coach Boeheim dismissed this argument. "If Carmelo stays one year, that's better than no years," he said. "For everyone involved." Anthony did receive his due from some sportswriters. Mike DeCourcy of the *Sporting News*, for instance, expressed the opinion that "Anthony played the college game better than any freshman in NCAA basketball. Ever."

In any case, Anthony enjoyed his college experience, which involved living a normal student lifestyle and sharing a modest apartment with one of his teammates. "I know a lot of people thought I was crazy to be here, but I liked it," he stated. "I just went out, played hard every game, enjoyed college for this one year. After that it's another decision." After completing his freshman year at Syracuse, Anthony decided to give up the remainder of his college eligibility and make himself available for the 2003 NBA draft.

NBA—The Denver Nuggets

Anthony was selected third overall—behind high-school sensation LeBron James and Serbian seven-footer Darko Milicic—by the Denver Nuggets. He joined a struggling franchise that had tied for the worst record in the league the previous season, at a dismal 17-65, and had not reached the playoffs since 1995. Before he even stepped on the court, Anthony won over Denver fans by praising the city and waiting to sign his 3-year, $8.67 million contract so that the team would have more money to acquire free agents.

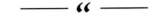

Anthony soon proved his value on the court, as well. During the first game of his rookie season, he led the Nuggets to victory over the defending NBA champion San Antonio Spurs. He went on to start every game of the 2003-04 season, averaging 36.5 minutes per game. He led the Nuggets in scoring with 21 points per game, and he also contributed 2.8 assists and 1.2 steals. Thanks to the impressive play of their rookie small forward, the Nuggets posted a vastly improved 43-39 record and earned a spot in the

"As a good player in the inner city, you're always hearing people say you're better than you really are and that you don't have to do things like everybody else," Anthony explained. *"When I was in Baltimore I took all that talk and ran with it. It distracted me from my schoolwork. I started getting suspended."*

playoffs for the first time in nine years. Unfortunately, Denver was knocked out in the first round by the Minnesota Timberwolves. Anthony won all six Rookie of the Month awards in the Western Conference, but the NBA Rookie of the Year Award went to LeBron James.

Playing in the Olympic Games

Following his successful rookie NBA season, Anthony joined the U.S. Men's National Basketball Team that played in the 2004 Olympic Games in Athens, Greece. Although he was thrilled to represent his country in international competition, he joined a group of relatively young, inexperienced players that had little opportunity to practice together before the Games.

As the Olympic tournament got underway, Anthony clashed with Team USA Coach Larry Brown, who had a reputation for being hard on young players. When Anthony complained publicly about his lack of playing time, Brown responded by limiting his minutes even further, to an average of 6.7 per game. Brown also informed the media that he found Anthony to be selfish and lazy. Anthony took the criticism personally and told a reporter that he could not wait for the Games to be over. "I'm not saying I'm the greatest player in the world, but I've never sat on nobody's bench," he declared.

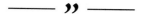

> *"I had a mentality that whoever doesn't believe in me, then screw 'em," Anthony acknowledged. "I'd go to practice, have an attitude the whole time, wouldn't talk to nobody."*

The American men lost an unprecedented two games in the first round, but they still managed to advance to the medal round. After beating Spain in the quarterfinals, however, Team USA lost in the semifinals to the eventual gold medal winner, Argentina. The Americans then defeated Lithuania to claim a bronze medal. Although Anthony found his Olympic experience disappointing, he said that it "motivated me to come back here [to Denver] and try to prove people wrong, that I'm not the person they portrayed me to be."

Struggling with Off-Court Controversies

Unfortunately, the period following the Olympics marked the lowest point of Anthony's basketball career. He returned to Denver for the start of the 2004-05 NBA season feeling frustrated and stressed out, and his poor attitude affected his relationship with his teammates. "I had a mentality that whoever doesn't believe in me, then screw 'em," he acknowledged. "I'd go to practice, have an attitude the whole time, wouldn't talk to nobody."

Next, a series of off-court incidents brought Anthony more bad publicity. In October 2004, he was arrested at Denver International Airport when security personnel found a small bag of marijuana in his backpack before he boarded the Nuggets' team plane. He immediately proclaimed his innocence. "He passed every drug test with the Nuggets because he does not take illegal drugs," said his lawyer, Daniel Recht. "The case has upset

Anthony is guarded by LeBron James of the Cleveland Cavaliers, December 2003.

Carmelo a great deal because he does not want his fans, especially the kids, to get the wrong impression of him." The drug possession charge was eventually dropped when one of his friends took responsibility for leaving the marijuana in Anthony's backpack.

The following month, however, the media obtained a video that showed Anthony fighting with another man at a New York City nightclub. He explained that the brawl occurred after the man spit a drink on his girlfriend, MTV personality La La Vazquez. Later, three other men were arrested for trying to force Anthony to pay them $3 million not to release the video of the incident.

—————— " ——————

"I was on top, and then everything was turning so bad," Anthony related. "I felt like the whole world was against me. I started isolating myself. I stopped talking to people, even my family. I was in a shell. . . . I was down, man. Really, really down."

—————— " ——————

In December 2004 Anthony became involved in yet another controversy when he appeared in a street video called *Stop Snitching*. The video showed footage of Anthony in his old Baltimore neighborhood hanging out with a group of men, some of whom were alleged drug dealers. It seemed designed to intimidate law-abiding people and prevent them from informing the police about drug dealing and other illegal activities. Anthony insisted that he had nothing to do with the video and did not support its message. "I'm completely against drugs and violence—that's not me," he declared. "I've lost friends to violence. I would never support anybody harming anyone."

Anthony realized that the negative publicity from these incidents threatened to destroy his reputation and even his career. "I was on top, and then everything was turning so bad," he related. "I felt like the whole world was against me. I started isolating myself. I stopped talking to people, even my family. I was in a shell. . . . I was down, man. Really, really down."

Sitting Out the All-Star Game

The first half of the 2004-05 season was tough for Anthony, as the pressure of dealing with off-court controversies, along with a nagging ankle injury, limited his production. The Nuggets struggled as well, posting a 17-25 record. These factors contributed to Anthony being left off the Western Conference roster for the NBA All-Star Game, which was held in Denver. Anthony's teammates knew that he would feel disappointed by this turn of events. "It may be a little tough for him," said Nuggets center Marcus Camby, "considering last year people were saying he should have been the rookie of the year and not LeBron because we made it to the playoffs. You look at this season, everybody's talking about LeBron and Dwyane Wade and they're barely mentioning Carmelo."

Anthony demonstrated some maturity by showing up for media events and watching the All-Star Game from the sidelines. "I made myself watch guys I play against every day—guys I could beat up on every day—play on my home court," he recalled.

Anthony is blocked by Chris Wilcox of the Los Angeles Clippers, March 2005.

"Laughing, joking. And I wasn't down there with them, knowing that I should have been." Anthony seemed determined to overcome his disappointment and focus on the future. "When people think of me, they think of me like I've been in the league 9, 10, 11 years," he noted. "This is only my second year. All-Star Game or not, I've still got plenty of time."

Turning His Life Around

Both Anthony and the Nuggets started to turn their fortunes around in the second half of the 2004-05 season. Anthony got help from Kiki Vandeweghe, Denver's general manager and a former NBA star, and from Kenyon Martin, a free agent guard who joined the Nuggets. Anthony began meeting with Vandeweghe for extra shooting drills, and the two men also spent a great deal of time discussing the personal challenges of playing professional basketball. "We talked a lot about what's important and where the passion is for him. He was getting away from that at the beginning of the year," the general manager recalled. "Sometimes when you have a setback or when you don't achieve the goal you want, that can drive you even harder. I think he's starting to realize that hard work is what's really going to get him over the top."

Shortly after Martin arrived in Denver, he realized that Anthony was struggling to deal with the leadership role he was expected to play on the team. The veteran took the second-year star aside and provided words of encouragement and support. "One day Kenyon pulled me up and said, 'You look like a lot of stuff is on your mind. I just want to tell you I'm on your side,'" Anthony remembered. "That conversation really turned everything around for me, because from that point on I knew that somebody had my back."

Inspired by his general manager and teammate, Anthony worked hard, lost weight, and regained his shooting touch. He also rekindled his love for the game and became more assertive on the court and in the locker room. "It just took me time to figure things out," he explained. "I had to learn the hard way. But I learned."

In the meantime, the Nuggets hired a veteran head coach, George Karl, who gave the young team more discipline and direction. With Anthony leading the way, Denver posted a 32-8 record in the second half of the season and returned to the playoffs. Unfortunately, the Nuggets were eliminated in the first round once again, this time by the San Antonio Spurs. Anthony averaged 20.8 points, 5.7 rebounds, and 2.6 assists per game on the year.

Anthony continued to improve over the course of the 2005-06 season. He gradually grew more comfortable with Karl's coaching style and expectations, and he incorporated some of the coach's criticism into his game to become a more complete player. Anthony increased his scoring average by 5.7 points per game to average a career-high 26.5, making him the eighth-leading scorer in the NBA for the season. He added a respectable 4.9 rebounds, 2.7 assists, and 1.1 steals per game. He also established a reputation as one of the best clutch players in the league by making five game-winning shots in the last 10 seconds of play. Despite his strong performance, however, he was passed over for the All-Star Team once again. The Nuggets finished the season in their usual fashion, posting a 44-38 record and getting knocked out in the first round of the playoffs by the Los Angeles Clippers.

Starring for Team USA

During the summer of 2006, Anthony rejoined the U.S. Men's National Basketball Team for the World Championships in Japan. From the time the team started practicing, he impressed the Team USA coaches with his hard work and leadership. "I got phone calls after the third practice of the USA team telling me he's the hardest worker, he's going to be captain of the team," said Nuggets Coach George Karl. "Four days before that, I had people say he wasn't going to make the team."

During the World Championship tournament, Anthony led Team USA in scoring with 19.9 points per game. Although the Americans posted an 8-1 record, they were forced to settle for another bronze medal after losing to Greece in the semifinals. Unlike the last time Anthony had faced international competition, though, no one questioned his level of desire and effort. "Carmelo was the ultimate team player. He had an outstanding summer, starting with our training camp in Las Vegas and ending with being a dominant player in the FIBA World Championships," said Team USA Coach Mike Krzyzewski. "I love the way he plays the game, but I love the way he carries himself as a leader on the Senior National Team even better." In recognition of his strong performance, Anthony earned the 2006 USA Basketball Male Athlete of the Year Award.

Making Another Mistake

Anthony's outstanding play continued when he rejoined the Nuggets for the start of the 2006-07 NBA season. He led the league in scoring through mid-December, averaging 31.6 points per game. But then he was involved in another damaging incident—this one on the court. It occurred during a game against the New York Knicks at Madison Square Garden. The Nuggets were leading by a comfortable score of 123-100 with just over a minute remaining to play. Some of the Knicks' players and coaches were upset that Anthony and several other Denver starters remained in the game even though the outcome had been decided. They felt that the Nuggets were being unsportsmanlike and running up the score.

> *"Carmelo was the ultimate team player," said Team USA Coach Mike Krzyzewski. "I love the way he plays the game, but I love the way he carries himself as a leader on the Senior National Team even better."*

When Nuggets guard J.R. Smith drove toward the basket, Knicks reserve player Mardy Collins grabbed him around the neck and slammed him to the ground. Smith got up and confronted Collins about the flagrant foul, and New York reserve Nate Robinson came over and pushed Smith away from his teammate. Robinson and Smith then began exchanging punches and fell into the courtside seats. Just as it appeared that the referees and coaches were getting the situation under control, Anthony approached Collins—the player whose hard foul had started the brawl—and dropped him to the floor with a punch to the face. Another Knicks player, Jared Jeffries, followed and threatened Anthony until security guards subdued him.

Television footage of the brawl was replayed over and over on news programs and sports shows across the country. Many fans and analysts were very critical of Anthony's behavior in the incident. The following day, NBA Commissioner David Stern announced the league's penalties for all of the players involved. Anthony received a 15-game suspension—the harshest punishment handed out in the incident, and the sixth-longest suspension in NBA history. "We judged him on his actions on the court," said Stern, "and they deserved a harsh penalty." Six other players were suspended for a total of 42 games, and each team received a fine of $500,000.

Anthony issued a public apology for his role in the brawl. During his suspension, he was allowed to practice with the Nuggets but he could not travel with the team or appear in games. He found the long mid-season layoff very hard to take. "This has probably been the toughest [thing I've been through]," he noted. "As I was going through all of that stuff I went through a couple of years ago, I still had a chance to get out on the court and play." Anthony was grateful for the continued support of fans, which helped raise his spirits during the suspension. "Everywhere I go, the majority of kids, they tell me I'm still their hero, I'm still their role model, and they can't wait until I get back out there on the court," he stated. "That gets my day going."

The Nuggets attempted to make up for the loss of Anthony by trading for Allen Iverson, one of the top guards in the NBA. Nevertheless, Denver struggled to 7-8 record without the young star leading the way. When Anthony finally got back into the Nuggets' starting lineup in late January, he was determined to learn from his mistake and become a better player and person. "I try to tell myself we all make mistakes. And this is a mistake," he said. "I have to put it in the past. One thing I learned from this is you always gotta think before you act. You can't just go out there and do something and then not think about the consequences until a couple of days later."

Finally Becoming an All-Star

Many observers felt that Anthony's suspension would hurt his chances of making the 2007 All-Star Team. When the Western Conference roster was announced, Anthony learned that he had been passed over once again in fan voting and in coaches' selections. As it turned out, though, NBA Commissioner David Stern added him as a reserve when several other players were unable to appear due to injury. Anthony was thrilled to finally make

After the disappointment of being left off the All-Star Team in earlier years, Anthony was finally selected for his first All-Star game in 2007. He scored 20 points.

Anthony and his mother, Mary, pose with children at a Christmas party at the Cross Community Coalition Family Resource Center in Denver. Anthony has been a big supporter of the Family Resource Center organization.

the All-Star Team in his fourth professional season. "Any way you can get in there is a blessing," he stated. "For me to be able to get in there—injury or votes or coaches' pick—it didn't matter."

Anthony entered the All-Star Game toward the end of the first quarter and went on to score 20 points to help lift the West to victory. "When I heard my name [announced], I told myself this was the validation of all the hard work I put in," he related. "Just to hear my name out there with the other guys, I was excited. I don't think I've been this excited in a long time."

Anthony continued to play well after the All-Star break. His scoring average of 28.9 points per game ranked second in the NBA, behind only Kobe Bryant of the Los Angeles Lakers. He also contributed 6.0 rebounds, 3.8 assists, and 1.18 steals per game. The Nuggets finished the year with a 45-37 record and made the playoffs, only to lose in the first round to San Antonio once again.

Despite the occasional mistakes that have marked his career, Anthony is still widely recognized as one of the best young players in the NBA. He possesses the speed, ball-handling ability, and outside shot to play on the perimeter, but at 6 feet 8 inches tall and 220 pounds, he also has the size and strength to be a force under the basket. This unique combination creates problems for opposing defenses.

Anthony's offensive skills have also made him one of the most popular players in the NBA, and his jersey often ranks among the best-sellers in all of sports. Given the challenges he has overcome in his life and career, he hopes to serve as an inspiration for his many fans. "Everyone will have bumps in the road, so you need to stay focused," he stated. "I'm here to tell you to stay strong. Don't give up. No matter what, today is a new chance."

MARRIAGE AND FAMILY

Anthony is engaged to be married to Alani "La La" Vazquez, an MTV video jockey, rap artist, and actress of Puerto Rican descent. They have a son, Kiyan, who was born on March 7, 2007. Anthony and his family live in a 12,500-square-foot mansion in Lakewood, a suburb of Denver. The home features an indoor basketball court, a batting cage, a recording studio, and a large garage to hold Anthony's collection of classic muscle cars from the 1960s and 1970s.

HOBBIES AND OTHER INTERESTS

In his spare time, Anthony enjoys watching classic TV shows and mafia movies. He is a big fan of the Baltimore Ravens football team and the Baltimore Orioles baseball team. Anthony also enjoys auto racing, and he is the co-owner of an Indy Racing League team with Ron Hemelgarn.

Anthony supports a number of charities, especially ones that help underprivileged children. For instance, he acts as a spokesperson for Family Resource Centers, a Colorado organization that helps poor families. "I came from an area where I saw poverty and hardship, and Family Resource Centers makes a big impact in helping people in those situations," he explained. "If I can make a difference in my community to help people who are struggling, then in the long run, it will make my career more fulfilling."

Anthony also spent $1.5 million to purchase and renovate a former Boys and Girls Club facility in Baltimore. When it reopened in 2007 as the Carmelo Anthony Youth Center, it provided hundreds of children with new after-school recreation and education options, including a gym, computer lab, dance studio, library, and meeting space. "There's nothing wrong with giving back," Anthony stated. "I was one of them kids years ago."

WRITINGS

Carmelo Anthony: It's Just the Beginning, 2004 (with Greg Brown)

HONORS AND AWARDS

First Team High School All-American (*Parade*): 2002
First Team High School All-American (*USA Today*): 2002
National Freshman of the Year (U.S. Basketball Writers Association): 2003
NCAA Final Four Most Valuable Player: 2003
NCAA First Team All-American (*Sporting News*): 2003
ESPY Award for Best Male College Athlete: 2003
Olympic Men's Basketball: 2004, bronze medal (with Team USA)
World Championship Men's Basketball: 2006, bronze medal (with Team USA)
USA Basketball Male Athlete of the Year: 2006
NBA All-Star Team: 2007

FURTHER READING

Books

Anthony, Carmelo, with Greg Brown. *Carmelo Anthony: It's Just the Beginning,* 2004 (juvenile)
Contemporary Black Biography, Vol. 46, 2005

Periodicals

Current Biography Yearbook, 2005
Denver Post, Dec. 15, 2006, p.D1; Jan. 21, 2007, p.B1
Denver Rocky Mountain News, Nov. 1, 2006, p.C1; Feb. 10, 2007, Sports, p.1
Esquire, Jan. 2005, p.76; Dec. 2005, p.118
Sports Illustrated, Apr. 16, 2003, p.24; Dec. 20, 2004, p.91; Mar. 27, 2006, p.50
Sports Illustrated for Kids, May 1, 2004, p.50

Online Articles

http://www.usatoday.com/sports/basketball/nba/nuggets/2005-02-07-carmelo-second-year_x.htm
(*USA Today,* "Star Nugget Anthony Aims to Regain Shine," Feb. 7, 2005)
http://www.usabasketball.com/seniormen/2006/06_aoy_anthony.html
(*USA Basketball,* "Carmelo Anthony Honored as USA Basketball's 2006 Male Athlete of the Year," Jan. 16, 2007)

Online Databases

Biography Resource Center Online, 2007, article from *Contemporary Black Biography,* 2005

ADDRESS

Carmelo Anthony
Denver Nuggets
1000 Chopper Circle
Denver, CO 80204

WORLD WIDE WEB SITES

http://www.carmeloanthony.com
http://www.nba.com
http://www.usoc.org
http://www.suathletics.com

Regina Carter 1963?

American Jazz Violinist
Winner of the 2006 MacArthur "Genius" Award

BIRTH

Regina Carter was born in Detroit, Michigan. She does not reveal her age, but her birthday is believed to be August 6, 1963, although some sources say 1966. Her father, Dan Carter, worked for the Ford Motor Company, and her mother, Grace Williamson Carter, was a kindergarten teacher. Carter has two older brothers, Danny and Reginald.

YOUTH

Carter's parents were not musical themselves, although they insisted their children receive a well-rounded education that included the arts. Carter began piano lessons at age two after surprising her brothers' piano teacher by playing back a melody by ear. However, her extreme youth made lessons problematic. At her first recital she changed the ending of the song she played. When her teacher corrected her, instead of playing it right, the little girl hit the wrong note over again, only with more emphasis. She recalled, "I just hammered down the note I had played before—like, 'No, this is the one *I* want to play.'"

———— " ————

Carter champions the Suzuki method for children, saying, "Children are not always taken with an instrument; they want to play something right away. So if they can play a tune right away, then you've got them. Otherwise it's not music; it's exercise."

———— " ————

The piano teacher suggested that a Suzuki violin program might be more conducive to Carter's creativity and her uncanny ability to play by ear. Suzuki is a method developed in Japan in the mid-20th century that uses young children's natural ability to learn new things as a basis for music instruction. The Suzuki method was created by Shinichi Suzuki, a Japanese musician and teacher who created a music education program to reflect his belief that talent can be nurtured in every child. (For more information on Suzuki, see *Biography Today*, Sep. 1998.) Carter's mother enrolled her at the Detroit Community Music School, which had recently begun offering the program. She was then four years old.

For the next eight years the young musician attended a weekly solo lesson after school one day each week and a group lesson from 8:00 to 3:00 on Saturday. She later recalled that the teacher used a variety of methods to help the students learn how to improvise songs and to read music. In one exercise, the teacher would create a melody line and then call on one of the students to add a line to follow. That student would play until the teacher called on another student, who would take over and continue to develop the song. Describing the exercise, Carter said, "So it was improvisation. . . . I think that really got me started on being free from the paper, making up things." To further develop the students' music knowledge, her violin teacher gave each student classical music records to take home and listen to each week. Carter now champions the Suzuki method for children, saying, "Children are not always taken with an instrument; they want to play something right away. So if they can play a tune right away, then you've got them. Otherwise it's not music; it's exercise."

As a child, Carter led a busy life. In addition to school and violin lessons, she continued with piano and also took tap and ballet. She enjoyed violin more than her other lessons, and by age 12 she planned a career as a soloist with a symphony orchestra. Her parents fully supported her aspirations, but playmates in her neighborhood wondered at her dedication. Many of the other students in her violin program, however, were the children of professional musicians. Through her close association with these families Carter gained further insights into musical technique and the life of a performance musician. As a teenager she trained in the youth program of the Detroit Symphony Orchestra. From time to time visiting musicians provided master classes to the young students, and Carter had the opportunity to participate in workshops taught by such renowned classical violinists as Itzhak Perlman and Yehudi Menuhin.

EDUCATION

Carter attended Cass Technical High School, a magnet school in Detroit. The school is known locally as Cass Tech and has a rich history dating back to 1861. Famous alumni of the school include the singer Diana Ross, the comedian David Alan Grier, and the musician Jack White, among many others. At Cass Tech, the music program was rigorous. In addition to violin, Carter took viola, oboe, and choir. She performed with a chamber group and the school orchestra. At Cass Tech she befriended fellow student Carla Cook, who went on to become a successful jazz singer and with whom Carter collaborated on the 2006 CD *I'll Be Seeing You: A Sentimental Journey*.

At that point Carter was following a musical education that would prepare her for a career in classical music. But occasionally the young musician would add her own ideas into the music as she practiced. According to the violinist, her mother would always call to her from another room, "Regina, that doesn't sound like your lesson to me."

From Classical to Jazz

After studying classical music for years, Carter became acquainted with jazz as a teenager. In classical music, the performers follow a musical score and play each note as it is written, including the timing and emphasis of the notes. The song will sound essentially the same when played by different musicians at different times. In jazz music, performers play the song in a unique way each time it is performed by using variations of the melody

and the notes that comprise the chords. Musicians also might alter the timing of notes to achieve different effects or work in fragments of other songs. The basic melody often remains intact and is repeated to give the tune a recognizable structure.

As Carter began listening to jazz, her music took off in a new direction. Through friends at Cass Tech she began listening to the works of violinists Jean-Luc Ponty, Noel Pointer, and Stuff Smith. She was particularly inspired after attending a concert by the French jazz violinist Stéphane Grappelli at a jazz festival in Detroit. Carter was excited by the way Grappelli improvised onstage and by the interplay among the band members. She later recalled the impact the concert made on her as a musician. "He was having such a good time, and I felt really elated after that. I said, 'If I could feel this way all the time, that would be it.' So that's what jazz meant to me. That feeling."

While still in high school Carter began performing with the Detroit-based funk band Brainstorm. She continued her high school classes and traveled with the band on weekends. After graduating from Cass Tech, she planned to prepare for a career as a classical musician and enrolled in the music program at the New England Conservatory in Boston, Massachusetts. But her interest in jazz was growing, and after a year she transferred from the classical music department to jazz. Unfortunately, the school did not have a program for jazz violinists, and her background left her unprepared for college-level theory courses.

Carter decided to transfer to another school. She returned to the Detroit area and entered the jazz music program at Oakland University in Rochester, Michigan. There she was taught by Marcus Belgrave, a jazz trumpeter who is well known in the Detroit jazz community. He often invited current and former students to play along with professional musicians in an informal setting at his house. Through Belgrave Carter met the organist Lyman Woodard and others active in Detroit's jazz scene.

"When I first starting playing jazz, I really didn't understand the music," Carter remembered. "I felt like jazz was some kind of big secret. Unlike classical music, you couldn't study books one, two, and three and then you've got it. I found out you have to study the culture of the music as well in order to learn jazz." Jazz professor and baritone saxophonist Marvin "Doc" Holladay told her not to listen to other violin players too much "because you're so new at this you'll start to sound like them." He told her, "Only listen for pleasure." Instead he suggested that she listen to horn players to hear how they phrase the music and pause for breath. Carter completed her music studies and graduated from Oakland University in 1985.

CAREER HIGHLIGHTS

After college, Carter taught strings in the Detroit public schools. Each week, through a program sponsored by the Detroit Symphony Orchestra, she visited schools that didn't have an orchestra teacher. Before long, however, she decided that a change of scenery would help her develop as an artist. She headed to Europe, spending the next two years in Germany. With her instrument Carter instantly made friends. In a music club on her first night in Munich she asked a jazz band if she could sit in with them to play on a tune. By the end of the night she had made a number of connections in the German jazz scene and gotten a lead on an apartment. During her stay in Germany she performed with various groups. She also spent time listening to records by saxophonist Charlie Parker and trying to imitate his solos on the violin. For a while she worked as a nanny for a German family and taught violin on a U.S. military base.

In 1987 Carter returned to Detroit and joined an all-female jazz band called Straight Ahead. The group achieved some success. They recorded two CDs and were invited to play at the Montreux, Jazz Festival in Switzerland. But she eventually decided that her chances of making it in the music industry would be improved by moving to the center of the jazz recording industry—New York City. And in 1991 she did.

Success in New York

Carter was well known in Detroit among jazz musicians, but in New York she was unknown. She was open to different musical styles and she needed to earn a living, so she performed everything from pop to country while establishing herself. Over the years she was hired to accompany a variety of performers, including Aretha Franklin, Lauryn Hill, Mary J. Blige, Billy Joel, and Dolly Parton. Still, nothing could compare with jazz, which she played with Oliver Lake, Max Roach and the String Trio of New York. Carter worked with that group on three CDs—*Intermobility* (1993), *Octagon* (1994), and *Blues . . . ?* (1996)—before leaving the trio to pursue a solo career. Her first individual effort, *Regina Carter*, was released in 1995 on Atlantic Records.

— " —

"[I don't] approach the violin as a violin; I approach it as a jazz instrument. The minute you approach it as a violin, it has a stereotype about it and ways that you're supposed to play it. I've gotten rid of all those ideas."

— " —

During the late 1990s Carter began solidifying her reputation as a technical, if unorthodox, musician with a unique appeal. *Something for Grace*, released in 1997, is an album dedicated to the artist's mother, Grace. In a favorable review, Hilarie Grey claimed that the songs soar and described Carter's style on the CD as "an aggressive, elemental approach to the violin." Critic Mike Joyce was equally positive. Particularly citing the cuts "Soul Eyes," "Listen Here," and "I'll Write a Song for You," he praised the album like this: "With both her pen and bow, Carter is able to imbue her music with rhythmic spirit and an all-embracing spirituality." During 1997 she toured with Wynton Marsalis's production *Blood on the Fields* and was featured in a solo that garnered attention from the press and made an indelible impression on audiences.

Building on these successes Carter changed record companies, signing with the Verve Music Group in a contract that allowed her more artistic freedom. *Rhythms of the Heart* (1999) was her first CD issued by Verve. This release saw her moving away from the smooth jazz presented on her earlier CDs. *Rhythms of the Heart* includes a reggae arrangement of the Motown classic "Papa Was a Rolling Stone" featuring singer Cassandra Wilson and the up-tempo "Lady Be Good" that drew comparisons to her forebear Grappelli. Critics responded to the adventurous energy of the collection, which showcased her wide repertoire and technical virtuosity.

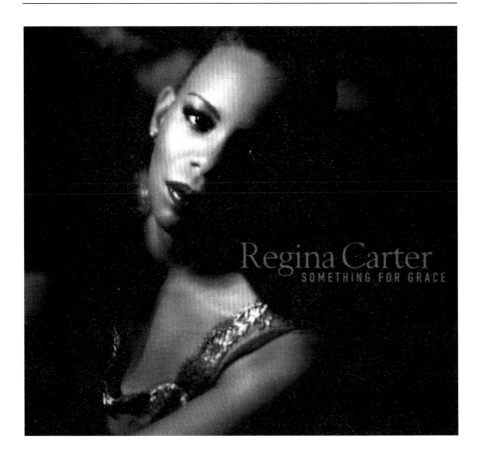

Released in 2000, *Motor City Moments* presents an homage to her hometown. Carter enjoyed selecting the songs for the CD, each one written or performed memorably by an artist with a connection to Detroit. She told an interviewer at the time, "This was a fun project. You should have seen one corner of my apartment. It was piled high with material . . . but it all boiled down to two factors: the piece had to speak to me on my instrument, and I had to feel that I could add something of my own to it." Works included Stevie Wonder's "Higher Ground" and Marvin Gaye's "Don't Mess with Mister T." Performers on the record included many musicians Carter knew from her early career in Detroit, including Belgrave on trumpet and her second-cousin James Carter on saxophone.

Playing the Cannon

In December 2001, Carter received an offer of a lifetime. The city of Genoa, Italy, invited her to play the Cannon (Il Cannone), one of the most famous

Carter playing the Guarneri violin, known as the Cannon. The violin was made in 1743 by Guarneri del Gesu and owned by composer Niccolo Paganini.

violins in existence. The instrument is named for the "explosive" sound that can be achieved on it. It was crafted in 1743 and was bequeathed to the people of Genoa in 1840 upon the death of its owner, the Italian composer Niccolo Paganini. The Italians extended their invitation to Carter as a gesture of solidarity in the aftermath of the terrorist attacks on New York City and Washington DC on September 11, 2001. Carter was both the first jazz musician and the first African American to play the Cannon. The concert in Genoa on New Year's Eve 2001 was an unprecedented success, and Carter received permission to record a CD using the Cannon.

That CD, *Paganini: After a Dream*, was recorded in 2002 and released in 2003. It includes both classical compositions by Maurice Ravel and Claude DeBussy and more contemporary works, including "Cinema Paradiso" by the Italian composer Ennio Morricone. Reviewers praised her performances on the recording for bringing out the expressive sound of the violin over a range of musical styles. Carter, too, was pleased with the results. At the time she said, "I love this recording and not just because of being able to use this violin, but because there was so much magic happening when we recorded the music. You could just feel the energy in the room and many of the tunes were recorded on the first takes. It was really, really scary and we thought, 'Wow, what's happening, like what's going on here?'" Carter played a farewell concert with the Cannon in New York City in November 2003 before returning the priceless instrument to the city of Genoa.

I'll Be Seeing You: A Sentimental Journey, Carter's sixth CD as a solo artist, was released in 2006. The album was conceived as a tribute to her mother, who had recently passed away. The song list includes her mother's favorites as well as other American standards from the 1920s to 1940s. In addition to "I'll be Seeing You," the CD includes renditions of Duke Ellington's "Blue Rose," Les Brown's "Sentimental Journey," and Ella Fitzgerald's "A Tisket, A-Tasket." The CD includes an original waltz by Carter titled "How Ruth Felt." Carter wrote this song as an expression of gratitude to Ruth Felt, an advocate of the performing arts in San Francisco, who helped support Carter through her mother's final illness. Carter has noted that she doesn't compose music often, but when she does, "it's more on a personal level. . . . I don't have a strong theory background, I have to wait for it to come to me and it can take a long time. At times I'll just sit there and think, 'OK, any day now,' just waiting for some idea to drop from the sky. There can be days where nothing happens and I have to accept that."

The MacArthur "Genius" Award

In September 2006 Carter received one of the most famous awards in the United States—a MacArthur Fellowship, also known as a "genius grant." These awards are given annually by the John D. and Catherine T. MacArthur Foundation, an organization that is "dedicated to helping groups and individuals foster lasting improvement in the human condition." To do this, they identify individuals whose creativity and past accomplishment suggest a successful future. The selection committee told Carter they had been watching her for three years before awarding her the prize. The award includes a grant of $500,000 over five years, enough to allow the winners the financial independence to pursue further creativity. The awards committee had this to say about her achievement:

"Regina Carter is a master of improvisational jazz violin. Though her work draws upon a wide range of musical influences—including Motown, Afro-Cuban, swing, bebop, folk and world music—she has crafted a signature voice and style. . . . Carter's performances highlight the often overlooked potential of the jazz violin for its lyric, melodic, and percussive potential. Her early training as a classical musician is reflected in the fluidity, grace, and balance of her performance. Carter's repertoire retains a firm connection with the familiar while venturing in new, unexpected directions. . . . Through artistry with an instrument that has been defined predominantly by the classical tradition, Carter is pioneering new possibilities for the violin and for jazz."

Carter planned to use the prize money to continue her education in music therapy. She noticed during her mother's illness that her vital signs improved when certain music was played. Carter hoped to explore the therapeutic value of music and develop a program to share with medical professionals. "Doctors are just now starting to embrace using music to help heal their patients," she explained. "I want to work with people who have learning disabilities or terminal illnesses. There are other things I can do than just performing. Music is not just entertainment."

During the time covered by the MacArthur Fellowship Carter also hopes to compose a new piece: she plans to take the poetry of Leslie Reese and set it to music in a work called *Black Bottom. Black Bottom* was the name of an African-American neighborhood in Detroit that was demolished in the 1960s to make way for urban renewal projects and a freeway.

> ————— " —————
>
> *"I don't think that a lot of us chose to be musicians. I didn't. It chose me. I think it's my job. I consider myself, in a way, to be a healer or to deliver a message. I definitely think it was a gift, and I don't believe in slamming the door on a gift."*
>
> ————— " —————

Hard Work and Success

Even though practice has been a part of her daily routine since she was a small child, Carter still struggles sometimes. She leaves her instrument in the middle of the bedroom at night so that in the morning it will be among the first things she sees. Typically she does warm up exercises on open strings and scales before working on the finer points of her technique. She still takes lessons to improve her understanding of jazz theory. She has said that the secret to her technique is that she doesn't "approach the violin as a violin; I approach it as a jazz instrument. The minute you approach it as a violin, it has a stereotype about it and ways that you're supposed to play it. I've gotten rid of all those ideas."

Asked about her decision to become a musician, Carter responded, "I don't think that a lot of us chose to be musicians. I didn't. It chose me. I

Carter working with a student on technique.
A natural teacher, she often visits schools when on tour.

think it's my job. I consider myself, in a way, to be a healer or to deliver a message. I definitely think it was a gift, and I don't believe in slamming the door on a gift." The important thing about jazz as an art form to her is "that it's a music of the people, like a voice. . . . It allows you to be creative and to take chances without having to know what the outcome is going to be and that's really the beauty of it."

Part of Carter's appeal is that her style of improvisation is enriched by many musical influences developed over the years. Her music draws techniques and sounds from diverse types of music, including classical, Motown, Middle Eastern, African, and Caribbean. She has attributed this to her upbringing in Detroit, with its rich musical history and ethnic diversity. She experiments with different sounds on the violin, incorporating bowing and pizzicato (plucking the strings), but also trying different techniques like hitting the strings with the back of the bow (the wood). Lowell Pickett, the owner of a jazz club in Minneapolis, Minnesota, believes that audiences respond so well to Carter's performances because they share in the happiness she expresses onstage. "She's a great player," he told *Strings*, "and she's so much fun. You can tell the way she just dives into the music and pulls out everything she can and then just throws it at the audience in a way that lets them share in the joy that she's feeling."

Summarizing the impact of Carter on jazz music, author Wayne Enstice described her as follows: "A fiddler who can make her four strings sing, swing, and cry the blues, Regina Carter is the most significant violinist to emerge on the jazz scene in decades." Guitarist Rodney Jones, who has performed with Carter, said this: "Regina's at the right place at the right time. She's unique because she can play mainstream jazz with authority, and she has the ability to interpret a ballad with so much emotion and nuance. She paints with the fine strokes of a master painter."

MARRIAGE AND FAMILY

Carter married Alvester Garnett in Detroit, Michigan, on September 5, 2004. Garnett plays the drums in Carter's band. Because they work together and she is his boss, the couple maintains a strict separation between their professional and personal lives. They don't even share a hotel room when the band travels on the road to performances. Carter says that helps "keep the professional distance, and it keeps the lines from blurring. And when we get home, we are really happy to see each other and do un-band-related things."

HOBBIES AND OTHER INTERESTS

Carter is active in music education and is pursuing studies in music therapy. She visits numerous schools across the country each year when she is on tour. She has been described as a natural teacher who easily connects with children. At Olympic Hills School in Seattle, Washington, principal Zoe Jenkins welcomed her visit: "There are 18 different languages represented at our school, but everybody here speaks music. . . . Music teaches focus, self esteem, a strong work ethic and self-expression. That's why we're so happy to have Regina here." Carter believes that music can have a positive impact on people. She has said, "Since I was a child, I've believed that there would be less angst, prejudice, and ignorance if everyone learned to play an instrument. We're all so guarded, but I know that when I play my violin, people can hear and see my real, complete self."

SELECTED RECORDINGS

As a Solo Artist

Regina Carter, 1995
Something for Grace, 1997
Rhythms of the Heart, 1999

Motor City Moments, 2000
Paganini: After a Dream, 2003
I'll Be Seeing You: A Sentimental Journey, 2006

With Straight Ahead

Look Straight Ahead, 1992
Body and Soul, 1993

With the String Trio of New York

Intermobility, 1993
Octagon, 1994
Blues . . . ?, 1996

With Kenny Barron

Freefall, 2001

HONORS AND AWARDS

MacArthur Fellowship (John D. and Catherine T. MacArthur Foundation):
2006

FURTHER READING

Books

Contemporary Black Biography, Vol. 23, 1999
Contemporary Musicians, Vol. 22, 1998
Enstice, Wayne and Janis Stockhouse, *Jazzwomen: Conversations with Twenty-One Musicians,* 2004
Peterson, Lloyd, *Music and the Creative Spirit: Innovators in Jazz, Improvisation, and the Avant Garde,* 2006
Stokes, W. Royal, *Living the Jazz Life: Conversations with Forty Musicians about Their Careers in Jazz,* 2000

Periodicals

Atlanta Journal-Constitution, June 27, 2004, p.JJ3
Billboard, Apr. 3, 1999
Current Biography Yearbook, 2003
Detroit Free Press, Aug. 30, 1998, p.E1; Jan. 11, 2004, p.G1; Sep. 19, 2006
Detroit News, Nov. 12, 2003, p.D1
Down Beat, June 1999, p.20; Apr. 2003, p.34; Oct. 2006, p.26
Essence, July 2003, p.98
Jazz Times, July/Aug. 1999
Jet, Dec. 1, 2003, p.24

Los Angeles Times, Sep. 26, 1999, p.9; Feb. 14, 2001, p.B6
Michigan Chronicle, July 5, 2006, p.D2
Minneapolis Star Tribune, Apr. 9, 2004, p.E5
New York Times, Jan. 2, 2002, p.E2; Nov. 2, 2003, p.B17; Sep. 12, 2004, p.I17
Orange County Register, Jan. 12, 2007
O, The Oprah Magazine, Apr. 2002, p.93
San Francisco Chronicle, Sep. 12, 1999, p.46
Seattle Post-Intelligencer, Sep. 11, 1999
Time, July 26, 1999, p.76
Utne Reader, Jan./Feb. 2001, p.98
Washington Post, Feb. 20, 1998, p.N10

Online Articles

http://www.allaboutjazz.com
   (*All About Jazz,* "Regina Carter: Improvising a Life in Jazz," Feb. 18, 2006)
http://jazztimes.com
   (*Jazz Times Magazine,* "Regina Carter: Something for Grace," June 1997)
http://jazzusa.com
   (*JazzUSA.com,* "A Conversation with Violinist Regina Carter," 1999; "Relating Her 'Motor City Moments': Regina Carter," 2000; "Regina Carter Interview: Queen of the Jazz Violin," 2006; "Interview with Regina Carter," undated)
http://www.npr.org
   (*NPR,* "Regina Carter's Encounter with a 'Cannon,'" May 14, 2003; "Musicians in Their Own Words: Regina Carter," May 19, 2005; "Jazz Violinist Regina Carter: 'I'll Be Seeing You,'" June 21, 2006)
http://www.stringsmagazine.com
   (*Strings,* "Motor City Maverick," Feb./Mar. 2002)

Online Databases

Biography Resource Center Online, 2007

ADDRESS

Regina Carter
Verve Music Group
1755 Broadway
New York, NY 10019

WORLD WIDE WEB SITES

http://www.vervemusicgroup.com
http://www.reginacarter.com

Kortney Clemons 1980-

U.S. Army Veteran and Paralympic Athlete
Winner of the 100-Meter Sprint at the 2006 U.S.
Paralympic Track and Field Championships

BIRTH AND YOUTH

Kortney R. Clemons was born on June 23, 1980, in Meridi-
en, Mississippi. Throughout his childhood, he spent much
of his spare time playing sports. "I always loved sports," he
recalled. "I always wanted to be part of a team." He particularly enjoyed playing football, and he spent hours practicing his moves in the backyard with his father, Mitch
Clemons. Although Kortney was always small for his age,

he was also fast and strong, which helped him excel at the position of defensive back.

EDUCATION

Clemons attended The King's Academy in Meridien, where he was a solid player on the school's baseball, basketball, and football teams. After graduating from high school in the late 1990s, he went on to attend East Central Mississippi Community College. Disappointed that his small size prevented him from playing college football, he decided to quit school and join the U.S. Army. He attained the rank of sergeant and served as a combat medic in the Iraq War. Following his discharge from the military, Clemons returned to school in January 2006. He enrolled at Pennsylvania State University, known as Penn State. His field of study is therapeutic recreation, and his career goal is to work with disabled athletes.

CAREER HIGHLIGHTS

Serving in the Iraq War

After leaving college in the early 2000s, Clemons enlisted in the U.S. Army. He initially hoped to receive training to become a pharmacist. Instead, the army gave him basic medical training to enable him to treat wounded soldiers in combat situations. He earned the rank of sergeant in the First Cavalry Division and was sent overseas to serve as a combat medic in the Iraq War.

This conflict began in March 2003, when the United States launched a military attack against the Middle Eastern nation of Iraq. President George W. Bush claimed that the war was necessary to prevent Iraqi dictator Saddam Hussein from arming international terrorist groups with weapons of mass destruction. The U.S. war effort succeeded in removing Hussein from power within a few short weeks, but American troops did not find any evidence that Iraq possessed chemical or nuclear weapons.

In the months and years following the U.S. capture of the Iraqi capital of Baghdad, it became increasingly clear that the war had created many problems in Iraq. The Iraqi people struggled to reconstruct their country and establish a democratic government in the face of violent postwar confrontations between rival religious and ethnic groups. Security became a serious concern as Iraqi insurgents and foreign fighters launched a series of attacks against American troops, international aid workers, and people connected to the new Iraqi government. These attacks became more sophisticated and deadly as the U.S. occupation of Iraq dragged on.

This was the situation Clemons faced when the U.S. Army sent him to Iraq, and he witnessed the effects of the continuing violence many times in his work as a combat medic. Just a few days before he was scheduled to return home, Clemons himself became a casualty. On February 21, 2005, his patrol came across an overturned U.S. Army vehicle on a dirt road outside Baghdad. It had run over a roadside bomb that had been placed there by insurgents. Clemons rushed to assist the driver of the vehicle, who had been wounded in the blast. As he prepared the soldier to be evacuated by helicopter, however, a second bomb exploded nearby. The explosion killed three fellow medics and inflicted serious wounds to Clemons's legs. "I crawled to the other side of the road where my friends were, and they covered me up," he remembered. "I was sitting, talking to them, and they were trying to keep me alert."

Clemons was evacuated to the U.S. military hospital in Landstuhl, Germany. When he woke up several hours later, he knew that something was wrong. "My cousin, who was in the military, came in and told me that I would see my family soon and that I needed to understand what had happened before they saw me," he recalled. "'You have to be strong for them,' she said. I lifted up the blankets and for the first time looked down where my leg had been." The injuries to Clemons's right leg had been so severe that doctors were forced to amputate the limb above the knee.

Clemons became a casualty of the war when a bomb exploded and inflicted serious wounds to his legs. "I crawled to the other side of the road where my friends were, and they covered me up," he remembered. "I was sitting, talking to them, and they were trying to keep me alert."

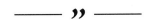

Coming to Terms with His Loss

As soon as he recovered from the surgery to remove his leg, Clemons was shipped back to the United States. He immediately entered a rehabilitation program for injured veterans at the Brooke Army Medical Center (BAMC) in San Antonio, Texas. Clemons worked hard physically to adapt to his disability. Within a few days of his arrival at BAMC, he began trying to walk again. He also had to learn new strategies for accomplishing everyday tasks that he had once done without thinking, like getting into and out of the shower safely. "It was like starting all over," he explained. "It was like a new beginning for me."

Clemons is one of the many amputees who has been treated at Brooke Army Medical Center (BAMC) in San Antonio, Texas.

In some ways, though, Clemons found it more difficult to adjust to the loss of his leg mentally than physically. "In the very beginning, you're happy you're still alive, but after that wears off, you hit the period of 'Why me?'" he acknowledged. "I had so many plans." Clemons felt particularly disappointed when he thought that his days of playing sports could be over. "Serving my country worked in my favor," he noted. "I kind of got stronger and quicker, and I was looking forward to coming back and at least playing softball or basketball here or there."

It took some time for Clemons to come to terms with his injury. He struggled to face his disability with determination and optimism and to find a way to feel normal again. "I had to reintroduce myself to myself," he stated. "When I was in the hospital, I thought I must have done something really bad in my life to deserve this. I went over everything that had happened to me, searching for a reason why God would want to take my leg. I came to the realization that He did this for a reason. He wanted me to make something more of myself. I had to lose my leg to find the real me."

In April 2005, just a few weeks after he arrived at BAMC, Clemons received some of the inspiration he needed to face the challenge of living with one leg. He saw John Register, a fellow amputee and head of the Paralympics Military Program, running around a track on his prosthetic leg. Even though Clemons was still learning to walk at that time, he was thrilled to discover that he might be able to run again someday. "I was so excited I couldn't sleep that night," he remembered. "I knew I could do this. I knew that I could accomplish great things."

Using Advanced Prosthetic Limb Technology

Before he could accomplish his goal of running, Clemons had to be fitted for a special prosthetic leg. The technology behind artificial limbs has advanced rapidly in the 21st century. Experts in prosthetic devices use computers to take three-dimensional measurements of the amputee's residual limb. They use these measurements to mold a custom socket that fits the stump perfectly. The other side of the socket connects to the prosthetic limb, which is likely to be made of carbon fiber or other advanced materials that are strong, yet lightweight and flexible. Many artificial limbs are battery powered, while others feature hydraulic shock absorbers or sophisticated electronic sensors.

Given his interest in running, Clemons was fitted for a "sprinter" leg. It consists of a thin carbon-fiber calf section and a metal flat-spring foot that curves up in the front like a sled. It also features a mini hydraulic system in the knee joint. The socket contains tiny electronic sensors that connect to Clemons's thigh muscles. These sensors detect which muscles are working in the front or back of his thigh, and then send messages to a computer chip that instantly adjusts the hydraulic joint to compensate. This system was designed to give Clemons the maximum balance and speed for running. Similar custom limbs have allowed other amputees to ride bicycles, ski, and engage in a variety of other activities.

In the near future, Clemons and other amputees may benefit from further exciting advances in prosthetic technology. Experts predict that it soon will become possible to connect artificial limbs directly to the bone in an amputee's residual limb. They also believe that new technology will allow electronic sensors to be attached to nerve endings, enabling amputees to control their prosthetic limbs with their brains. All of these advances have

Clemons stretches after a workout at the Multisport Indoor Facility at Penn State.

helped change the way that doctors view amputation. "Rather than being considered a treatment failure, [amputation] is viewed by our staff as one of the treatment options aimed at maximizing the soldier's rehabilitation potential," declared Colonel Mark Bagg, chief of orthopedics and rehabilitation at BAMC.

Only six months after sustaining his injury, Clemons ran for the first time at BAMC. He compared the sensation of running on his prosthetic "sprinter" leg to hopping on a pogo stick. Even though it felt different, Clemons found the experience exhilarating. "I had tried it for a few strides before that moment, but I had never gone full speed," he recalled. "I took off down the track, and it was the most wonderful feeling, the wind in my face, moving by my own power."

Becoming Involved in the Paralympics

Almost as soon as Clemons began running, he started dreaming about competing in the Paralympic Games. This international athletic competition for disabled athletes was founded in England following World War II, as a way to give injured war veterans a chance to compete in sporting events. Like the Olympic Games, it is held every four years and features the top athletes from around the world. In fact, the competition takes place in the same location and uses the same facilities as the Olympics, but it is generally held a few weeks later. The U.S. Paralympic Team placed fifth overall at the 2000 Games in Sydney, Australia, and fourth at the 2004 Games in Athens, Greece.

Organizers of the American Paralympic program understand that they tend to get a larger pool of disabled athletes to draw from during times of war. This is particularly true of 21st century conflicts like the Iraq War, because U.S. soldiers are less likely to die in combat than in previous wars. Whereas 24 percent of wounded American troops died from their injuries during the Vietnam War in the 1970s, this number has decreased to 10 percent during the Iraq War. Analysts attribute the declining death rate to the development of body armor made of Kevlar, a form of lightweight plastic that is five times stronger than steel. Worn in the form of a vest, Kevlar protects soldiers' bodies and vital organs from bullets and shrapnel.

Unfortunately, Kevlar is too bulky for soldiers to wear on their entire bodies. The technology protects their torsos—and thus reduces the number of combat deaths. But it also leaves their extremities exposed—and thus increases the number of limb injuries and amputations. Making the most of a bad situation, soldiers who are injured in combat can provide a good source of athletic talent for the U.S. Paralympic Team. "We have a population of young amputees who were very fit and very athletic before they got wounded," said Captain Justin LeFerrier, who manages the physical therapy facility at BAMC. "Our job here is to get them back to whatever level they want to get to. If they've lost both legs and want to run, they'll run. As far as we're concerned here, the word impossible just means it hasn't been done yet."

> *"People in Iraq are still getting injured every day, and if I can give them something to strive for, [show them] that it can be done, give them some type of hope, that would be my greatest accomplishment," Clemons stated. "The more I can help someone else, it gives me more energy to keep going."*

The U.S. Paralympic Team launched a special program, called the Paralympic Military Summit, so the growing number of injured Iraq War veterans could become involved in disabled sports. The program encourages the veterans to take up sports in order to relearn skills, build confidence, and return to a healthy, active lifestyle. During a three-day training session, they get to participate in such events as wheelchair fencing, sitting volley-

Getting ready to race at Penn State.

ball, and sled hockey. "These types of sports allow us to know we might have bad days, just like anybody else, but we can continue to move on in life and still compete," Clemons noted. "You can't get stuck in that rut, start feeling pity for yourself, and let life pass you by."

Clemons attended a Paralympic Military Summit in Colorado in October 2005. Although less than a year had passed since his injury, he was inspired to begin training to compete in the 100-meter sprint event at the 2008 Paralympic Games in Beijing, China. Since he had done a lot of weightlifting in the army, Clemons also began training for the Paralympic powerlifting event.

Inspiring Other Injured Veterans

In January 2006, when Clemons enrolled at Penn State, he had the opportunity to work with some of the top coaches in adaptive sports as part of the school's Ability Athletics Program. By May, he was ready to compete in the powerlifting event at the 2006 International Paralympic Committee World Championships in Korea. Clemons set a new U.S. Paralympic record of 340 pounds in the 155-pound senior division. He placed 11th overall and qualified for the 2008 Paralympics in the event.

In the meantime, Clemons continued improving his skills on the track. In July 2006 he became the first Iraq War veteran to compete in the U.S. Paralympics Track and Field National Championships, which were held in Atlanta, Georgia. This event would help determine the U.S. team for the 2008 Paralympic Games. Clemons won the national championship in the 100 meters with a personal-best time of 15.61 seconds. Although he was thrilled to qualify for the 2008 Paralympic Games in a second event, he was more excited about setting a good example for other injured veterans. "I'm not in this to beat other people," he explained. "I just want to set records. There are a lot of guys who have come back from Iraq like me. I want them to look at those records and see what is possible. I'm living proof that you can accomplish anything."

Clemons hopes that a strong showing at the 2008 Paralympic Games in Beijing will also help motivate people facing similar challenges. "People in Iraq are still getting injured every day, and if I can give them something to strive for, [show them] that it can be done, give them some type of hope, that would be my greatest accomplishment," he stated. "The more I can help someone else, it gives me more energy to keep going."

HOME AND FAMILY

Clemons, who is single, lives and trains on the campus of Penn State University. He has a ten-year-old daughter, Daytriona.

AWARDS AND HONORS

U.S. Paralympics Track and Field National Championships, 100-Meter Sprint: 2006, gold medal

FURTHER READING

Periodicals

Atlanta Journal-Constitution, June 30, 2006, p.A1
Current Science, Feb. 10, 2006, p.10
New York Times, Oct. 9, 2005, sec. 8, p.1
Soldiers Magazine, Mar. 2006, p.28
USA Today, Nov. 21, 2006, p.C3

Online Articles

http://www.msnbc.com.msn.com/id/13051084
   (*MSNBC.com*, "Iraq War Amputee Seeks Track Success," June 20, 2006)

ADDRESS

Kortney Clemons
United States Olympic Committee
U.S. Paralympics Division
One Olympic Plaza
Colorado Springs, CO 80909

WORLD WIDE WEB SITE

http://www.usolympicteam.com/paralympics

Miley Cyrus 1992-

American Actress and Singer
Star of the Disney Channel Television Program
"Hannah Montana"

BIRTH

Miley Cyrus was born in Franklin, Tennessee, on November 23, 1992. Her birth name is Destiny Hope Cyrus, but she was such a happy baby that her dad called her "Smiley Miley," and the nickname Miley stuck. Her parents are Billy Ray Cyrus, a singer, songwriter, and actor, and Letitia "Tish" Finley Cyrus. Miley has five siblings: an older half-sister, Brandi, two older half-brothers, Trace and Christopher; a younger brother, Braison Chance, and a younger sister, Noah Lindsey.

YOUTH

Miley was born in the same year that her dad shot to stardom on the strength of his catchy, country-flavored tune, "Achy Breaky Heart." The song climbed to the No. 4 spot on the *Billboard* Hot 100 list in 1992 and was a mainstay of the line-dancing fad of the early 1990s. The album on which it appeared, *Some Gave All,* sold 14 million copies. Billy Ray Cyrus was never able to recapture the success of his first hit, but he has continued to record music and tour. Eventually, he became a television star, recognized around the world because of "Doc," a program broadcast on Pax TV. In it, Cyrus played a country doctor who works in New York City.

> *Even as a young child, Miley was convinced that she wanted a career in entertainment, just like her father. Billy Ray recalled, "Since she was little, she would look at me confidently and say, 'I'm going to blow by you, Daddy. I'm going to be a singer, songwriter, entertainer.'"*

Her dad's celebrity status taught Miley a lot about life in the spotlight—both the good and bad sides of it. It also gave her opportunities to get used to being in front of an audience. She always liked performing with her father. As a toddler, she would dash on stage during his concerts if she got the chance. When she did this, he would go along with it, singing a few duets with her before sending her back offstage.

Miley's love of performing lasted beyond her toddler years. As she got older, she became convinced that she wanted a career in entertainment, just like her father. Billy Ray recalled, "Since she was little, she would look at me confidently and say, 'I'm going to blow by you, Daddy. I'm going to be a singer, songwriter, entertainer.'" At first he discouraged her, knowing that show business can involve a lot of heartbreak. But Miley was persistent. When Billy Ray Cyrus began filming "Doc," he allowed her to act in a few episodes. These experiences gave her confidence and strengthened her feeling that show business was right for her. When her parents realized how determined she was, they allowed her to start taking lessons from an acting coach and going to auditions. They also gave her a Daisy Rock guitar, and she became an endorser for the company, which makes guitars especially for girls.

Cyrus with her father and the rest of the cast from "Hannah Montana."

Miley's experiences on "Doc" showed her "how much fun, joy, and encouragement there is on the set," she recalled. "It's great seeing everyone working together as a team on the show. You are all together and you're all a family and it's a really great place to be." In addition to her TV performances, Miley also worked in some music videos, had a part in the movie *Big Fish*, and appeared on another show her dad was involved with, "Colgate Country Showdown," a country music talent search.

EDUCATION

Because of her commitment to her TV show, Miley doesn't have time to attend regular school. She is tutored on the set of "Hannah Montana" in Burbank, California.

CAREER HIGHLIGHTS

"Hannah Montana"

Miley was 11 years old when she first auditioned for a new show being planned by the Disney Channel. The series would feature a middle-school age girl who is a pop superstar, but who hides her identity at school because she wants to have a normal life. Disney executives were eager to produce the show, but they knew they had to find the right actress to play the part before they could get started.

The Disney Company has proven to be very good at training young performers and managing their careers for maximum success. Justin Timberlake, Britney Spears, Hilary Duff, and Raven are just some of the entertainers who got a lot of experience and exposure at an early age on the Disney Channel. (For more information on these performers, see the following issues of *Biography Today*: for Timberlake, see N Sync in *Biography Today*, Jan. 2001; for Spears, see *Biography Today*, Jan. 2001; for Duff, see *Biography Today*, Sep. 2002; for Raven, see *Biography Today*, Apr. 2004.) In the case of Hilary Duff ("Lizzie McGuire") and Raven ("That's so Raven"), Disney first gave them lead roles in television. After they had gained an audience, the girls were launched on singing careers.

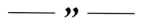

> "[The Miley Stewart character] is just like me, but she's also like any other average girl going through love stuff, friend stuff, and family stuff. But she is trying to get through the pressure of being a universal super star. Everyone loves Hannah, but she just wants to have her friends and her family."

"Hannah Montana," the new Disney show, would combine those two steps. Its star would have to be confident and funny enough to handle the comedy scenes in the show, and a strong enough singer to be a convincing superstar. According to Gary Marsh, the president of entertainment for Disney Channel Worldwide, "We decided we would not go through with this series until we found a kid who could carry a sitcom as well as she could carry a tune."

Perfect for the Part

Miley's first audition for "Hannah Montana" went well. Decision-makers at Disney thought she was a good actress and singer, and a stable, down-to-earth person. But they needed someone who could handle the pressures of life in the spotlight, and they thought that an 11-year-old probably would have a hard time dealing with the long hours and demanding pace of filming the show, making publicity appearances, and keeping up

Two views of Cyrus: as herself (left) and as Hannah Montana (right).

with schoolwork. Besides, Miley was small for her age, too small to play the part of a teenager. Although her audition was good, she didn't get the part.

A year passed, and Disney still hadn't found the right girl. The "Hannah Montana" show was on hold. "I kept going after this part, because it is really something I wanted to do," Miley remembered. When she was 12, she got another chance to audition. This time, she won the role. Gary Marsh praised Miley, saying, "She has the everyday relatability of Hilary Duff and the stage presence of Shania Twain, and that's an explosive combination." Miley was thrilled to have achieved her goal. "I've always loved singing, and I've always loved acting and dancing," she said. "Getting this opportunity with Disney, I get to do it all. They let you do everything you love." Miley and her family left their Tennessee farm and moved to California so she could work on "Hannah Montana" at the Disney studios there. Her grandmother stayed behind to look after their horses, dogs, and other pets.

There are some parallels between the life of Miley Cyrus and the setup of "Hannah Montana." In the show, Miley's character—a bubbly teenager named Miley Stewart—moves from Nashville to California to pursue her career. Unlike Miley Cyrus, however, Miley Stewart wants to keep her identity as Hannah Montana, the pop superstar, a secret. Only her two best friends know about Miley's other life; the rest of the students at Sea-view Middle School hardly notice her, even though most of them are huge fans of Hannah Montana.

Double Identity

"Hannah Montana" doesn't try to be particularly realistic. In the show, Miley just has to toss on her blonde stage wig and a little makeup to trans-form into Hannah, and her classmates don't seem to recognize her. Episodes involve such goofy antics as Miley spying on her dad while he picks out a dress for her, Miley parasailing in a chicken suit, and Miley being asked out on a date—to attend a Hannah Montana concert.

Comedy is an important ingredient in "Hannah Montana," but so is music. The show has lots of footage of Hannah in concert. To get it, Disney started by having Miley perform as Hannah at Walt Disney World. Though they already had confidence in her appeal, Disney executives were im-pressed by the way the crowd went wild over the singer. "They didn't know who she was. The show wasn't on the air yet, so that was another sign that we had something really, really special," said Adam Bonnett, an executive responsible for programming at the Disney Channel.

In addition to Miley, "Hannah Montana" features Billy Ray Cyrus in the role of her father and manager, a musician named Robbie Stewart. Also appearing are Mitchel Musso and Emily Osment as her friends Oliver and Lilly, and Jason Earles as her older brother Jackson. The character's mother is dead, but she has appeared on the show in a dream sequence, played by Brooke Shields. Other guest stars have included Jesse McCartney and Dolly Parton.

Success on TV and the Music Charts

"Hannah Montana" debuted in March 2006. That first show drew the biggest audience in the history of the Disney Channel—more than five million viewers. But that strong start was only the beginning. Disney gave Miley lots of support, featuring her music and videos on Radio Disney and the Disney Channel, which reaches more than 100 countries. She was the opening act on a 40-city tour with The Cheetah Girls, another popular Disney-produced group which, like "Hannah Montana," is aimed at the "tween" audience (children between 8 and 12 years old). Many types of Hannah Montana merchandise were created, including clothing, cosmet-ics, dolls, and video games.

Miley has had some success as a recording artist, including this CD soundtrack Hannah Montana 2: Meet Miley Cyrus.

That promotional effort paid off. "Hannah Montana" is consistently ranked as one of the most popular programs among girls ages 9 to 14, and it also has a huge following among younger children, both boys and girls. When a CD titled *Hannah Montana: Songs From and Inspired By the Hit TV Series* was released, it entered the Billboard 200 chart in the No. 1 spot. The CD featured eight songs by Miley and a few by other artists, including Jesse McCartney and The Click Five. Miley's contributions included the "Hannah Montana" theme song, "Best of Both Worlds," "Pumpin' Up the Party," "The Other Side of Me," "This Is the Life," and "Just Like You." The CD had seven singles on the *Billboard* Hot 100 at one time and sold 1.6 million copies in just two months. Sales eventually passed 2 million.

Miley is enjoying her success. "There's nothing more fun than being out on stage and getting the vibe from the crowd. There's nothing like being on a set where you are there to make other people happy and to make them laugh. That's the best job in the world," she said. She enjoys performing as Hannah, whose sound she has compared to that of singer and "American Idol" winner Kelly Clarkson. (For more information on Clarkson, see *Biography Today*, Jan. 2003.) But Miley wants to be recognized for her own musical style too. "I get on my own thing—a little country and then pop and rock and some bluegrass," she said. In 2007, she performed her own music and Hannah's on her second CD, *Hannah Montana 2: Meet Miley Cyrus*, which immediately rose to No. 1 on the pop charts.

———— " ————

"We have a good family," Miley said. "I still go to church every Sunday with my family and really just want to learn, because I don't want to blend in with everyone. I just want to give a good image and a good message to girls, and guys, too."

———— " ————

Miley on Miley

Describing the Miley Stewart character, she said, "Miley is just like me, but she's also like any other average girl going through love stuff, friend stuff, and family stuff. But she is trying to get through the pressure of being a universal super star. Everyone loves Hannah, but she just wants to have her friends and her family." As for why "Hannah Montana" is so popular, she said, "I think everybody has a goal or a dream, and just showing an average girl having her dream come true and still being able to balance her friends and her school is something they relate to."

Despite her fame and her apparent confidence, Miley admits that—like most teenagers—she sometimes feels very self-conscious. "I freak out," she said. "I look in the mirror and think, 'This shirt is ugly. These pants are stupid.' It's a lot easier when I have someone to put my makeup on and fix my hair. People on TV have a lotta people pulling it together for us. It makes all the difference. Honestly, I hate getting dressed up. I'm holding my shoes in most pictures you see of me at red-carpet events. If I could go to premieres in my sweats, I would!"

Being recognized wherever she goes has presented some challenges, but so far Miley likes it. Her father has always treated his fans well, and she wants to do the same. "Say 'hi' to me," she said. "I love it. Everyone I have a chance to take a picture with or sign an autograph for—just a quick way to make them smile—that's awesome."

HOME AND FAMILY

Miley lives with her family in California and works with her father on the set of "Hannah Montana." The chemistry between the two of them has been called one of the best things about the show, but she has said that working together isn't always easy. Discussing the daily drive to work with her dad, Miley joked, "I want to play my music and he just talks and talks about anything. Finally, I turn on my little iPod and let him talk to himself. I'm like any other teenage girl who doesn't necessarily want her dad around all the time. But—and I would never let him know that—he's really cool." Billy Ray Cyrus said that he and his daughter have always communicated best through their music: "Since Miley was a little girl we've been writing songs together. We sing together. We do a whole lot more of it off-stage than on stage," he said.

Miley knows that it can be hard to handle the pressures of fame, but she is confident that she can handle it, thanks to her strong family life and her faith in God. "We have a good family," she said. "I still go to church every Sunday with my family and really just want to learn, because I don't want to blend in with everyone. I just want to give a good image and a good message to girls, and guys, too."

HOBBIES AND OTHER INTERESTS

In her free time, Miley likes to shop, swim, play basketball, and go skateboarding. Before moving to California, she was active as a cheerleader. She enjoys horses and other pets. She is a vegetarian and likes Thai food, as well as cookie dough, Gummi bears, Cheetos, and candy.

SELECTED CREDITS

Television

"Hannah Montana," 2006-

Recordings

Hannah Montana: Songs from and Inspired by the Hit TV Series, 2006
Hannah Montana 2: Meet Miley Cyrus, 2007

DVDs

Hannah Montana: Livin' the Rock Star Life!, 2006
Hannah Montana: Pop Star Profile, 2007

Films

Big Fish, 2003 (as Destiny Cyrus)

HONORS AND AWARDS

Nickleodeon Kids Choice Awards: 2007, Favorite Television Actress, for
"Hannah Montana"

FURTHER READING

Periodicals

Boston Globe, Nov. 6, 2006, Metro section, p.A1
Fort Worth Star-Telegram, Feb. 13, 2007, p.E1
Girls' Life, Dec. 2006, p.47
Houston Chronicle, Mar. 4, 2007, Star section, p.1
Los Angeles Times, July 8, 2007, p.E1
New York Times, Apr. 20, 2006, p.E1
People, July 2, 2007, p.72
Philadelphia Inquirer, May 17, 2006
Time, Nov. 30, 2006
USA Today, Jan. 11, 2007, p.D1
Variety, Feb. 20, 2006, p.18

ADDRESS

Miley Cyrus
Disney Channel
Attn: Fan Mail Dept.
3800 West Alameda Ave
Burbank, CA 91505

WORLD WIDE WEB SITES

http://www.mileycyrus.com
http://tv.disney.go.com/disneychannel/hannahmontana

FALL OUT BOY

Andy Hurley 1980-
Patrick Stump 1984-
Joe Trohman 1984-
Pete Wentz 1979-
American Pop-Punk Band

EARLY YEARS

Fall Out Boy is a four-man pop-punk band that formed in 2001 in the suburbs of Chicago, Illinois. The members are Andy Hurley (drums), Patrick Stump (vocals and guitar), Joe Trohman (guitar), and Pete Wentz (bass and backup vocals).

Andy Hurley

Andrew John Hurley was born on May 31, 1980, in Menominee Falls, Wisconsin. His mother, Ann Hurley, is a nurse; his father died when he was five years old. Hurley attended Menominee Falls High School, where he gained a reputation as a gifted percussionist in the school band who was also a bit of a troublemaker. According to his mother, "He had a lot of anger in him as a youngster. . . . He was afraid to become close to people. A band to him was safe and was a family that wouldn't leave him." Before joining Fall Out Boy he attended the University of Wisconsin, Madison, where he studied history and anthropology. Hurley is a vegan (he doesn't eat or wear anything derived from animal products). In addition, like his band mates Patrick Stump and Pete Wentz, Hurley adheres to what is known as a "straight-edge" lifestyle. Straight edge is a commitment not to drink alcohol, smoke, or use drugs.

[The hardcore scene] focused too much on negative energy," said Wentz, "and that bogs you down after a while and gets really tiring."

Patrick Stump

Patrick Martin Stumph was born on April 27, 1984, in Glenview, Illinois. As a teenager, he changed the spelling of his last name from "Stumph" to "Stump" to prevent confusion about the pronunciation. His parents are Patricia Vaughn and Dave Stumph, an amateur folk musician who works as an association manager. They divorced when Stump was a child, and one of his earliest musical memories is of helping his father move his record collection out of their house. Stump has an older brother, Kevin, who is a violinist. Stump attended Glenbrook South High School and graduated in 2002.

Joe Trohman

Joseph Mark Trohman, the youngest member of Fall Out Boy, was born on September 1, 1984, in Hollywood, Florida. His father, Richard Trohman, is a cardiologist who moved the family to the Cleveland, Ohio, area when Joe was about five years old. Trohman attended Chagrin Falls Middle School and played trombone in the school band. He also took piano lessons and began playing guitar before the family relocated once again. When he was 12, they moved to the affluent North Shore suburbs of Chicago. There Trohman attended New Trier High School in Winnetka, Illinois, graduating in 2002. According to his father, "Joe did play guitar for hours upon hours

The members of Fall Out Boy (left to right):
Joe Trohman, Pete Wentz, Andy Hurley, and Patrick Stump.

from age eight or nine. . . . He got good fast. . . . Joe would wake up in the middle of the night and start playing."

Pete Wentz

Peter Lewis Kingston Wentz III was born on June 5, 1979. His father, Peter Wentz II, is a law professor, and his mother, Dale, is a private school administrator. Pete has a sister, Hilary, and a brother, Andrew. He attended New Trier High School before transferring to North Shore Country Day, a private school also in Winnetka. He excelled in soccer and was named to the all-state team during his senior year. After graduating from high school in 1997, Wentz attended DePaul University to pursue an interest in political science, but he soon dropped out to focus on music.

FORMING THE BAND

Fall Out Boy got started in the Chicago area, where all four members were involved in music. What brought them together was their shared interest in hardcore music. Hardcore derives from the punk rock genre that developed during the 1970s with such bands as the Sex Pistols in England and the Ramones in the United States. Songs are noted for being characteristically loud, fast, and short. The lyrics often express anger or dissatisfaction with the government or society.

The members of Fall Out Boy were all involved with various bands before starting their own, and they crossed paths at several points. Wentz, who is the oldest member of Fall Out Boy, had played in several hardcore bands in Chicago, including xfirtsbornx and 7 Angels of the Apocalypse. He was well known in the area as the lead singer of the band Arma Angelus. Wentz and Hurley played together in Arma Angelus and also in another band, Racetraitor, and Trohman toured one summer with Arma Angelus when he was just 16. After that, Trohman met Stump, who was also in a band, at a local bookstore where Stump worked. They were both high school juniors at the time. Trohman introduced Stump to Wentz, and the three of them began hanging out together and eventually began playing music together for fun.

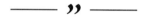

In Stump's opinion, "I don't consider it Fall Out Boy until Andy joined."

When they first got together, Wentz, Trohman, and Stump were just having fun pursuing a new musical direction. The music they developed was more melodic and less pessimistic than the intense, hard-driving music they had been playing in their other bands. According to Wentz, "[The hardcore scene] focused too much on negative energy and that bogs you down after a while and gets really tiring."

What started out as merely an amusing break from their other projects soon led to performances at local venues. But they had difficulty finding a drummer who fit well with the group. They began using the name Fall Out Boy after they asked for suggestions from the audience at one of their early shows. Someone in the crowd shouted out "Fall Out Boy," the name of a comic book that Bart reads on the animated television show "The Simpsons." The name stuck.

Eventually an early version of the group produced a CD titled *Evening Out with Your Girlfriend*. This 2002 release includes the songs "Pretty in Punk" and "Parker Lewis Can't Lose (But I'm Gunna Give It My Best Shot)." The band, however, has since disavowed this record. In interviews they've explained that its production and musical quality do not

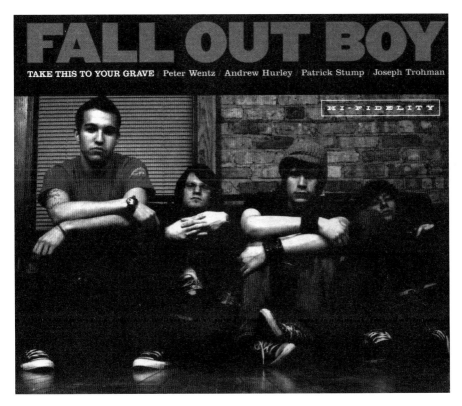

FALL OUT BOY

TAKE THIS TO YOUR GRAVE / Peter Wentz / Andrew Hurley / Patrick Stump / Joseph Trohman

HI·FIDELITY

Take This to Your Grave *was the first CD with the full lineup of Fall Out Boy.*

meet with the standards they hold for their work. Also, it was recorded before Hurley joined the band, so they don't regard it as a true Fall Out Boy CD. The band tried several drummers before Hurley joined Fall Out Boy in 2003 when they needed a replacement drummer to go out on tour. Stump surely spoke for the group when he said, "I don't consider it Fall Out Boy until Andy joined."

CAREER HIGHLIGHTS

With the lineup finally settled, Fall Out Boy worked hard touring, writing songs, and recording new music. Hoping to be signed to a recording contract, they uploaded MP3s to the web and submitted demos—self-recorded CDs that include a sample of the band's repertoire—to numerous record labels. In 2003 they signed with the Florida-based company Fueled by Ramen, which is co-owned by Vinnie Fiorello, the drummer of the band Less Than Jake. They also impressed Island Records, which advanced them money to pay for recording and touring expenses. Island also acquired the rights to sign the band if their first CD did well.

In 2003 Fall Out Boy released the CD *Take This to Your Grave* on the Fueled by Ramen label. The music was hard-driving and guitar based, revealing their past in the hardcore scene. But the lyrics and song titles were not filled with rage, as in much hardcore music, but were instead filled with irony, humor, and clever puns. Songs on the disc include "Reinventing the Wheel to Run Myself Over," "Tell That Mick He Just Made My List of Things to Do Today," "Homesick at Space Camp," and "The Pros and Cons of Breathing." Many of the songs were about a bad breakup between Wentz and his girlfriend.

Because of the personal revelation in the lyrics, Fall Out Boy became associated with emo, another music genre. Emo evolved from hardcore punk and is characterized by highly personal lyrics fraught with emotion. The term is usually used for bands and musicians who perform songs with confessional lyrics that are characterized by their emotional intimacy, intensity, and sincerity. But the music accompanying those lyrics can take a variety of forms, including both softer acoustic sounds and pounding rock with loud guitars and vocals.

———— " ————

According to Wentz, "When people come up to me and say 'Fall Out Boy saved my life,' my only response is that Fall Out Boy saved my life, too."

———— " ————

Through near-constant touring, Fall Out Boy built a loyal following of fans who knew the words to all the songs and sang with them at live performances. The band's outrageous stage antics drew even more people to its shows. Wentz is known for throwing his bass all the way around his neck and catching it, tossing the bass through the air, shaking his whole body like an electric current is shocking him, and diving from the stage to surf the crowd. Trohman and Wentz often electrify the audience by jumping off monitor cabinets. Describing the bassist's performance at a concert in Tempe, Arizona, reviewer Christina Fuoco wrote, "Wentz proved that original bass-playing styles can still be found and thrown into the mix; he seemingly strums all of the stings while still picking out the correct notes, while spinning around like a six-year-old child." The fans, too, can get wild at Fall Out Boy shows. At one performance the surging crowd pushed a female fan up against the stage so hard that her arm was visibly broken. Stump recalled, "She's like 'I'm not leaving until you play my favorite song,' so we were like, 'Let's play it as fast as we can. We have to get her to the hospital!'"

As their fan base and celebrity increased, the band released *My Heart Will Always Be the B-Side to My Tongue* in 2004. This package contained a five-song EP and accompanying DVD. Included on the music disc are acoustic versions of "Nobody Puts Baby in a Corner" (based on a line from the 1987 movie *Dirty Dancing*) and "Grand Theft Autumn." In addition the EP offers a cover of the Joy Division classic "Love Will Tear Us Apart." The DVD includes videos, concert footage, a slide show, and interviews.

At about this time Wentz was seeing a psychiatrist for depression; he was hospitalized in 2005 after taking too many prescription pills. His reasons for taking the pills are unclear, but he later said that he merely wanted to sleep, not to commit suicide. "I was isolating myself further and further," he said, "and the more I isolated myself, the more isolated I'd feel. I wasn't sleeping. I just wanted my head to shut off." Wentz has continued therapy and is a spokesperson for Half of Us, a campaign to help college students deal with depression. He credits the band with his own recovery. According to Wentz, "When people come up to me and say 'Fall Out Boy saved my life,' my only response is that Fall Out Boy saved my life, too."

From Under the Cork Tree

Fall Out Boy's next release, the 2005 CD *From Under the Cork Tree*, was a great success both musically and commercially. The singles "Dance, Dance" and "Sugar, We're Goin' Down" were among the biggest hits of the year on MTV and on such music web sites as I-Tunes and Napster.

In addition to the mega-hits, the CD again showcased the band's humor in such song titles as "Our Lawyer Made Us Change the Name of This Song So We Wouldn't Get Sued," "A Little Less 'Sixteen Candles,' A Little More 'Touch Me,'" and "Champagne for My Real Friends, Real Pain for My Sham Friends."

For the band, however, *From Under the Cork Tree* represented an artistic breakthrough, as well. During preparation of the CD they developed a new songwriting formula. For earlier efforts, singer Stump had written the lyrics and Wentz and the others developed the music to go along with them. On *From Under the Cork Tree* they reversed their roles. Wentz provided poetry to Stump, who then put the verses to music. Since that time this process has remained in place: Wentz writes the lyrics, Stump uses the Apple software GarageBand to develop a rough version of the

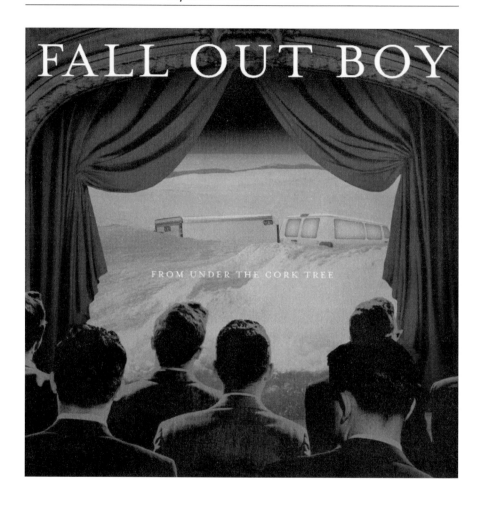

song, then the band refines it. Trohman praised Stump's creative ability, saying, "I guess Patrick is some kind of genius—he's a total mad scientist." Stump's mother, Patricia Vaughn, agreed that the band has success with this method. According to Vaughn, "Patrick is the sound of Fall Out Boy. . . . He's the guy that hears it, and Pete presents it. The combination of the two is the perfect storm."

Critics and audiences responded favorably to *From Under the Cork Tree*, which went on to sell more than three million copies. Hometown music journalist Jim DeRogatis of the *Chicago Sun-Times* raved, "Fall Out Boy boasts the hooks of a great pop-punk band, but it plays with the intensity of a hardcore group." The band even gained fans among music industry executives, including Jay-Z, the rapper and president of Island/ Def Jam Records, who went to see them when they played in New York. He said,

"Everyone knew the words and was singing. It was like a cult following. I watched them and thought, 'These guys are stars. This is genuine.'"

Awards soon followed. "Sugar, We're Goin' Down" won the MTV2 Award in 2005, and "Dance, Dance" won the MTV Viewers' Choice Award in 2006. At the 2006 Teen Choice Awards the group took prizes in three categories. Wentz and Stump accepted the honors on behalf of the group, but as usual, Wentz did the talking. "We always feel like we're kinda sneaking into these things. It's kinda like we're just getting away with it, I guess." He thanked all the fans who voted, especially the fans who posted messages for the band at their web site and all the fans who have started bands of their own. "You guys are awesome," he concluded.

Infinity on High

After the success of *From Under the Cork Tree*, the group's next release was highly anticipated. "The Carpal Tunnel of Love," the first track from the new album to be made public, was available in December 2006 as a download on I-Tunes and from absolutepunk.net. The first official single, "This Ain't a Scene, It's an Arms Race," was released in January 2007. *Infinity on High* debuted as the No. 1 album in the country in February 2007, selling more than half a million copies during its first month of re-

"Fall Out Boy is just an honest band with humble origins whose members are as surprised as anyone at their new-found success," said reviewer Chris Rolls.

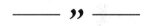

lease. The title of the CD is taken from a letter by the 19th-century Dutch artist Vincent Van Gogh, who wrote, "Be clearly aware of the stars and infinity on high. Then life seems almost enchanted after all."

Many reviewers commented on the album's clever and witty lyrics. The songs talk about the band members' personal struggles in a self-mocking, self-deprecating way, bolstering their reputation for sincerity. This approach has allowed the band members to hang on to their credibility as indie artists as they sell millions of records and forge deals with corporate sponsors. Many of the songs seem to poke fun at their celebrity while also seeming to enjoy it. They manage to combine sincerity with a sense of ironic detachment, what critic Jody Rosen called "songs that both wallow in and lampoon emo angst."

Reviewers also commented on a shift in the band's musical style, with more variation in tempo and clear R&B and traditional rock influences.

The songs on the CD take advantage of Stump's wide vocal range, including the gospel-inspired "Hum Hallelujah" and the melodic piano ballad "Golden." Critic Sasha Frere-Jones declared, "The album is deeply pleasurable, consisting of compressed, torqued-up rock songs that rarely detour into instrumental passages and return single mindedly to choruses that range from the reasonably hummable to the eminently hummable." "It's a natural progression," said Wentz. "It's our growth as songwriters and our experiences in the world. All of a sudden, our eyes have adjusted to the dark and we can see different things."

To achieve their new sound the band worked in the studio with producer Kenneth "Babyface" Edmonds and several guest artists, including Jay-Z and guitarist Ryan Ross of Panic! At the Disco. They wanted to work with Edmonds, according to Wentz, because the band appreciates "his approach to melody. . . . Patrick [sings] with a greater range and more soul in our new songs, and we wanted to find someone to drive that." Reviewer Barry Nicolson especially praised the uptempo "Don't You Know Who I Think I Am," calling it brilliant. With breaks punctuated by hand claps, Stump sings, "A penny for your thoughts / But a dollar for your insides / Oh, a fortune for your disaster / I'm, just a painter and I'm drawing a blank." According to Nicolson, "If you don't like it, you're either deaf or a liar."

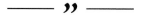

> "We mean a lot to each other as musicians and as people," Trohman admitted. "But sometimes we start believing what people write about us: That the band is just one guy or two guys. That can be harsh for the soul."

Celebrity and Success

The band's success has brought celebrity to some of its members, mostly to Wentz. Fall Out Boy breaks the typical patter for many bands. Stump is the lead singer, but he is not the public face of the band. Instead, Wentz is unquestionably the most visible member of the group—he does most of the media interviews, he's become a favorite of many pre-teen and teenage girls, and his every move is covered in magazines. He is also well known for his business pursuits outside of Fall Out Boy, including the record label Decaydance Records and the clothing line Clandestine Industries. Describing Wentz's drive for business, Stump has said, "It scares me sometimes, watching him. The two sec-

Fall Out Boy performing at the House of Blues in Chicago, 2007.

onds you're not with that dude he's made 30 decisions that are going to affect us for the rest of the year."

Stump has not seemed jealous of all the attention Wentz gets. "I don't know if my contribution is recognized, and I don't care," he declared. "I know what I do and I'm busy doing it. I'm not one of these guys who sets out to take charge of things. That's how Pete is: He's a born leader." Besides, according to Stump, he's "horribly uncomfortable with being the frontman." Trohman has indicated that the friendship at the core of the band helps. Still, he admitted that "We mean a lot to each other as musicians and as people. But sometimes we start believing what people write about us: That the band is just one guy or two guys. That can be harsh for the soul." According to Wentz, "In the vacuum away from all the press and away from all that camera flashing, we are still just best friends and that's how it will continue to be, I hope, all the way into the future."

Fall Out Boy has devoted a lot of time to connecting with their fans, including meeting them at shows, offering web-exclusive previews of their new material, uploading personal blog entries, and using message boards and personal networking sites to correspond with the public. Their MySpace page listed 1.8 million friends as of spring 2007. Sometimes when Fall Out Boy arrives early in a city for an arena show they announce a free afternoon show at a small club in the same town. They post a message online about where and when the surprise performance will take place, and fans spread the word through text messages and IMs. According to Wentz, "We feel indebted to our fans and will always try to pay them back."

Trying to explain their appeal, reviewer Chris Rolls has suggested that fans relate to the band because of the sincerity evident in their music. "Rest assured that this merry band of melodic, heavy-riff pop players is not a carbon copy of their contemporaries, nor are they a product of producers hell-bent on making a buck off popular trends. No, Fall Out Boy is just an honest band with humble origins whose members are as surprised as anyone at their new-found success." Wentz believes their audience responds to being treated with respect. "There is an honesty in our music and I think people appreciate it. We have never dumbed down to teenagers by writing songs about being in high school and having your locker jammed. . . . We have always written what we are really feeling. We have always had the respect that they are going to figure out these songs for themselves and come up with their own interpretations."

HOME AND FAMILY

When not touring with Fall Out Boy, Hurley lives in Germantown, Wisconsin. Stump still lives in Glenview, Illinois, and also owns a condominium in Los Angeles, California. Trohman lives in a townhouse in Chicago. Wentz lives in Los Angeles, California.

MAJOR INFLUENCES

In an interview in 2004, Wentz talked about the band's major influences. "In the beginning," he said, "it was The Descendants, Green Day, the Police, Elvis Costello. Now with our newer stuff it's like Joy Division, The Cure, Nick Drake—stuff like that. . . . We like a lot of hardcore too." Stump has mentioned Michael Jackson's album *Thriller* as well.

RECORDINGS

Evening Out with Your Girlfriend, 2002
Take This to Your Grave, 2003
My Heart Will Always Be the B-Side to My Tongue, 2004 (EP)
From Under the Cork Tree, 2005
Infinity on High, 2007

HONORS AND AWARDS

MTV Video Music Awards: 2005, MTV2 Award, for "Sugar, We're Goin' Down"; 2006, Viewers' Choice Award, for "Dance, Dance"
XM Nation Music Awards: 2005, "On the Rise" Most Important Mainstream Emerging Artist Award
Napster Awards: 2006, Most Played Song Award, for "Dance, Dance"
Teen Choice Awards: 2006 (three awards), Choice Single Award and Choice Rock Track Award, for "Dance, Dance," Choice Rock Group Award

FURTHER READING

Books

Contemporary Musicians, Vol. 57, 2005

Periodicals

Billboard, Jan. 27, 2007
Chicago Sun-Times, May 2, 2003, p.5
Chicago Tribune, Mar. 30, 2006, p.28
CosmoGirl, June/July 2006, p.102
Entertainment Weekly, Feb. 9, 2007, p.71
Independent (London), Apr. 28, 2006, p.12
Kansas City Star, Apr. 13, 2006, p.G7
Minneapolis Star Tribune, Apr. 14, 2006, p.F1
New Yorker, Mar. 12, 2007, p.86
People, Feb. 26, 2007, p.90
Rolling Stone, Nov. 30, 2006, p.17; Mar. 8, 2007, p.50

Spin, Dec. 2005, p.62; Mar. 2007, p.52
Teen People, June/July 2006, p.30

Online Articles

http://www.blender.com
  (*Blender*, "Boy Crazy!" June 2006)
http://www.cleveland.com
  (*Cleveland Plain Dealer*, "Fall Out Boy's Trohman Ready to Play 'Big Rock'
  at Blossom," May 18, 2007)
http://www.designerpunk.co.uk
  (*Designer Punk.co.uk*, "Interviews," Mar. 17, 2004)
http://www.livedaily.com
  (*LiveDaily*, "LiveDaily Interview: Fall Out Boy's Pete Wentz," Dec.14, 2006)
http://www.mp3.com
  (*MP3.com*, "Fall Out Boy: With or Without You," Apr. 10, 2006)
http://www.mtv.com
  (*MTV News.com*, "Pete Wentz: The Boy with the Thorn in His Side," May
  31, 2006)
http://www.nme.com
  (*NME.com*, "Fall Out Boy: *Infinity on High*," May 23, 2007)
http://www.onmilwaukee.com
  (*OnMilwaukee.com*, "Milwaukee Native Hurley Keeps the Beat for Fall
  Out Boy," May 17, 2007)
http://www.rollingstone.com
  (*Rollingstone.com*, "Let's Hear It for Fall Out Boy," Feb. 24, 2006; "The
  Boys with the Car Crash Hearts," Feb. 21, 2007)

Online Databases

Biography Resource Center Online, 2007, article from *Contemporary Musicians*, 2005

ADDRESS

Fall Out Boy
Island Records
825 Eighth Avenue
New York, NY 10019

WORLD WIDE WEB SITES

http://www.falloutboyrock.com
http://fueledbyramen.com
http://www.myspace.com/falloutboy
http://www.islandrecords.com

America Ferrera 1984-
American Actress
Star of the TV Series "Ugly Betty" and the Movie
The Sisterhood of the Traveling Pants

BIRTH

America Georgine Ferrera was born on April 18, 1984, in Los Angeles, California. Although her parents were born in Honduras, Ferrera and her five older siblings (four sisters and a brother) were raised by their mother in Woodland Hills, a district of Los Angeles located in the San Fernando Valley. "My mother decided to come to this country," she revealed, "for the sole purpose that my siblings and I could get an education, could have every opportunity in the business world, and whatever we wanted to pursue would be at our fingertips."

When America was seven, her parents divorced and her father returned to Honduras. Her mother raised her six children as a single mother, working as a director of housekeeping for the Hilton Hotels. "No matter how much a single mother makes, six mouths is a lot to feed," Ferrera said in praise of her mother, who is also named America. "And then to find time to raise them? I don't know how she did it. She's amazing."

YOUTH

Ferrera spent much of her early life feeling like an outsider. She grew up in Woodland Hills, a predominantly white area with a large number of Jewish residents. Many of her friends held bar and bat mitzvahs, the Jewish coming-of-age celebration that takes place when a girl turns 12 or a boy turns 13. "Where I grew up, I went to tons of bar and bat mitzvahs, and I've never been to a single quinceañera," she recalled, referring to the traditional Hispanic celebration when a girl turns 15. Still, Ferrera felt a deep connection to her cultural heritage. "When you are first-generation anything, you have your past, which is these roots, and it's a part of you because you're so deeply connected to your relatives," she explained. "But then you have the society that you're supposed to blend into." Her mother spoke Spanish at home, but Ferrera and her siblings would usually respond to her in English. "I understand Spanish and I can speak it, but not fluently," she admitted.

As a child, Ferrera never felt like she fit in with the Latino community, primarily due to where she lived. "All of my friends were white Jewish kids," she recalled. "So the Latino kids thought I was this white girl." At the same time, she felt distant from the other children at school. "As early as second grade I remember feeling really different and isolated," she said. "I had the hugest crush on a boy, and my best friend had a crush on him too. One day he said to me, 'I like your best friend more because she's paler and she has freckles.' And it was right then that I began to feel like, 'Oh wow, I'm different.'" Although she experienced feelings of loneliness at school, she was close with her siblings. "Growing up, I never had a ton of friends. I always had two or three, but when you have four sisters and a brother all a year apart, you don't really need anyone else to play with," she stated.

While her mother worked, Ferrera spent her time watching television and movies, developing an interest in acting from an early age. "As a child I knew acting was what I wanted to pursue. Being able to interpret a role and communicating what I feel is very satisfying to me." She began taking roles in school plays, and she also performed in local community theater groups. "My first play was *Romeo and Juliet*. I was in third grade, but I went to a junior high school and auditioned for the play," Ferrera remarked. "They gave me the part of the Apothecary, the druggist who gives Romeo the drugs to kill himself." Later, in the fifth grade, she played the role of the Artful Dodger in the school production of *Oliver*. At the age of 15, she enrolled in acting classes, which she paid for by waiting tables and babysitting. In addition to her interest in theater, she also became an avid reader, identifying with the Latino lives portrayed in the works of such authors as Sandra Cisneros and Julia Álvarez.

EDUCATION

At El Camino High School, Ferrera excelled in academics. She graduated in 2002 with a 4.3 grade point average and was named valedictorian, the student with the highest grade point average in her graduating class. Despite this success, she does not have fond memories of her experience at El Camino High School. "My high school days were definitely *not* the best days of my life," said Ferrera. "It was about hiding all the things that made me different and trying to fit in somewhere. I didn't know who I was."

"My high school days were definitely not the best days of my life," said Ferrera. "It was about hiding all the things that made me different and trying to fit in somewhere. I didn't know who I was."

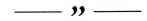

Ferrera entered the University of Southern California on a presidential scholarship, deciding to pursue a double major in theater and international relations. "Acting is something I knew I wanted to do long term," she declared. "But not going to college was not an option. I think it probably helped me as an actress as well, because actresses need real-life experiences to draw from." While attending college, she also continued to act professionally. Her college career was interrupted by the success of her TV show, "Ugly Betty." Ferrera is currently one semester shy of earning her degree, having taken the 2006-07 school year off to concentrate on the show. She plans to complete her education soon. "Once doing the show becomes more routine, I hope to fit in a class at a time and just slowly work toward my degree. I've come too far to quit one semester before graduation."

FIRST JOBS

According to Ferrera, her mother was reluctant to encourage her daughter to pursue acting professionally. "Acting was not something that they [my parents] came to this country to have me do," she said. "I don't think her fears came from thinking that I couldn't do it; she knew I had a passion and I really wanted to act. I think her fears came from her not being sure that I could make it in such a cruel business. . . . [She] wants security for me; she wants me to have a good life, and what I have had to do is prove to her that this is what the [good] life is for me." Despite her mother's skepticism about professional acting, her mother also counseled her on the importance of being proactive, advice which Ferrera has followed. "My mom told me that you have to be a go-getter. You have to go after what you want in life."

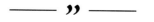

> "I never turned on the TV and saw a Latina woman with an average body," Ferrera revealed. "I thought, 'I'll never be a Charlie's Angel, because I can't fit into size zero leather pants.'"

Ferrera began attending auditions for acting parts while she was still in high school. But these first auditions were not successful, prompting her mother to suggest that she reconsider her career choice. "I said, 'You need to change your mind. You're short. You're Latino. You're not blond. You don't have blue eyes. You won't get into this business,'" her mother remembered. "She [America] said, 'You don't understand. I want to do this like a doctor wants to be a doctor, like a teacher wants to be a teacher.'" While she was still attending El Camino High School, Ferrera was signed by a small talent agency. After a year of rejections for commercial auditions, she landed a role in the 2002 Disney Channel television movie *Gotta Kick It Up!*

CAREER HIGHLIGHTS

While attending drama camp as a 16-year-old at Northwestern University in Chicago, Illinois, Ferrera shot a videotaped audition for a part in the 2002 independent film *Real Women Have Curves*. "I sent in the tape and then didn't think twice about it," Ferrera explained. "I just went back to enjoying my summer in Chicago." But the audition soon led to a part in what became her first major critical success.

Ferrera in a scene from Real Women Have Curves.

Real Women Have Curves

Real Women Have Curves was adapted from the play by Josefina Lopez and starred veteran Hispanic actors Lupe Ontiveros and George Lopez. Ferrera was cast as Ana, a first-generation Mexican American teenager living in East Los Angeles with her mother, Carmen, played by Ontiveros. Ana is torn between accepting a scholarship to Columbia University and working with her family at a garment factory.

The title of the film, which refers to Ana's acceptance of her physique, served as a source of identification for Ferrera as well. Speaking of her own self-image, she stated: "I never turned on the TV and saw a Latina woman with an average body and I thought, 'I'll never be a Charlie's Angel, because I can't fit into size zero leather pants.'" She had to overcome her insecurities for a scene in which Ana strips down to her underclothes in an act of defiance against her mother. "It was weird at first," Ferrera confessed. "It was like a room with 20 men, the crew. I had to be really confident for that scene. I had to forget about my own feelings." The theme of pride and confidence in oneself runs throughout the film. "You leave this movie feeling happy about who you are. And that's something we're all hungry for," she maintained.

Originally filmed for HBO, *Real Women Have Curves* caused a sensation at the Sundance Film Festival. Critics lauded Ferrera's performance, nominating her for an Independent Spirit Award for Best Debut Performance and a Young Artist Award for Best Performance in a Feature Film—Leading Young Actress, both in 2003. Along with costar Ontiveros, Ferrera won the Special Jury Prize for acting at the 2002 Sundance Film Festival. The movie was released in theaters in 2002.

After the movie came out, Ferrera had conflicting feelings about pursuing an acting career. But then an influential professor changed her perspective: "I couldn't see how it could be important in a world with so much war and hatred, where people are starving to death and dying. So I went to my favorite college professor for advice. He told me about how he mentored a young Latina girl who asked him to watch my movie *Real Women Have Curves* because she felt like the story reflected her life. She had always felt invisible in the world, but the movie changed her life by giving her a voice and a better understanding of herself. That made me feel so much better about what I do."

Plainsong

Ferrera got a chance to expand her range as an actress in the 2004 Hallmark Hall of Fame television movie *Plainsong*. Based on the best-selling

Ferrera with castmates from The Sisterhood of the Traveling Pants *(left to right): Blake Lively, Amber Tamblyn, and Alexis Bledel.*

novel by Kent Haruf, *Plainsong* revolves around the lives of simple towns-folk living in rural Colorado. The film features such notable actors as Aidan Quinn and Rachel Griffith. The character played by Ferrera, Victoria Roubideaux, is a pregnant teenager who has been kicked out of her mother's house. She is taken in by two kindly brothers who live alone on their farm. The movie contains a scene in which Victoria gives birth. "I wanted to make that as real as possible and I spent the most time trying to make that authentic," Ferrera explained. "I watched a lot of birthing videos, which were painful to watch." The experience made Ferrera think cautiously about her own life. "I told my mom she never has to worry about me getting pregnant," she added.

The Sisterhood of the Traveling Pants

In 2005, Ferrera landed one of the main roles in *The Sisterhood of the Traveling Pants*. The movie was adapted from the best-selling young adult novel of the same name by Ann Brashares, the first of several books in a series about a group of friends. *The Sisterhood of the Traveling Pants* stars Ferrera, Alexis Bledel, Blake Lively, and Amber Tamblyn as four teenage best friends. The group finds a pair of jeans in a thrift shop that magically fits them all despite differences in size and body type. In an effort to remain connected during a summer spent apart, each of the girls spends a week wearing the jeans, and then mails them to the next girl. Although the movie has a light touch, it deals with serious issues like divorce, death, and the loss of virginity. Ferrera's character, Carmen, is spending time with her father, who left her and her mother when she was a child. For her performance in the film, Ferrera was nominated for a 2006 ALMA Award for Outstanding Actress in a Motion Picture and a Teen Choice Award for Choice Movie Breakout Performance—Female.

——— " ———

"What is special about it is Betty is just a regular girl that appeals to all different races and all kinds of audiences—and she just happens to be Latina. And for a Latina character to be out there in a mainstream way and without a banner on her head is a true success and a step forward."

——— " ———

Ken Kwapis, the director of *The Sisterhood of the Traveling Pants*, spoke admiringly of Ferrera's performance. "For me, what's amazing about America's character, Carmen, is that she's the most verbally expressive of the four girls and yet her entire story is about not being able to say something. And it takes the better part of the picture for her to finally step up and tell her father how much her parents' divorce has hurt her. One of the beautiful things about America's work is that she's able to be completely expressive and yet you understand how on this one point she can't open up. In any case, her rawness is a major contribution to the film." Kwapis encouraged the young actresses to form a bond in real life that would mirror the friendship of their characters. "He gave us $75 each, Canadian dollars," Ferrera recounted, "and dropped us off at a vintage shop. This was our rehearsal. 'I want you guys to shop together.' We were like, we feel good as far as chemistry goes, but if you want to send us shopping we will go."

"Ugly Betty"

Ferrera's biggest success to date came with the starring role on the hit ABC television program "Ugly Betty." The series is based on "Yo soy Betty

Scenes from "Ugly Betty": Betty at home with her family at the dinner table (top); Betty in one of her notable outfits (center); and Wilhelmina (Vanessa Williams) undergoing a Botox treatment (bottom).

la fea," a popular Columbian telenovela, a type of Latin American TV show that is similar to a soap opera. One of the producers of "Ugly Betty" is the Mexican actress Salma Hayek, who appears on the show. The cast also features Eric Mabius, Ana Ortiz, Tony Plana, Rebecca Romijn, and Vanessa Williams.

Ferrera plays Betty Suarez, the assistant to an editor at a prominent fashion magazine. Everyone else at the magazine is gorgeous, perfect in their fashion sense and physical appearance. Betty's poor sense of style and distinct appearance (she has braces, oversized glasses, and thick eyebrows) make her an unlikely candidate for such a job. But her good humor and positive outlook help her boss improve his performance in the company, and "ugly" Betty is shown to be much more intrinsically beautiful than her perfect co-workers.

——— **"** ———

"When I'm in character and in Betty's costumes, I feel beautiful. I never feel as beautiful and confident in my real life. There's a light that shines from within. I love, love, love being her."

——— **"** ———

The show's enthusiastic response from audiences all over the world has been lauded as a milestone for Latin American women in popular media. "The fact that she's not blonde-haired and blue-eyed is, by itself, very much a big deal," San Francisco State University professor Melissa Camacho stated. "We've been waiting a long time for a TV character who looks like her and has her voice." Ferrera also sees the character of Betty in this unique light. "What is special about it is Betty is just a regular girl that appeals to all different races and all kinds of audiences—and she just happens to be Latina," she claimed. "And for a Latina character to be out there in a mainstream way and without a banner on her head is a true success and a step forward rather than have a token Latin show for Latinos by Latinos."

Ferrera and has said that she wholeheartedly enjoys her work on the show and has expressed her admiration for the character of Betty. "When I'm in character and in Betty's costumes, I feel beautiful. I never feel as beautiful and confident in my real life. There's a light that shines from within. I love, love, love being her." Tony Plana, the actor who plays Betty's father, considers her a natural fit for the role. "Acting for America is like breathing," he said. "She's naturally layered and complex." Critics agreed. Ferrera was honored with the 2007 Golden Globe Award for Best Performance by an Actress in a Television Series in the Musical or Comedy. That same year, she also received the Actor Award from the Screen Actors Guild for Outstanding Performance by a Female Actor in a Comedy Series.

Other Television, Film, and Theater Work

In 2005 Ferrera had a small part in the 1970s skateboarding film *Lords of Dogtown*, which dramatizes the true story of three teenage surfers from Venice Beach, California, who take an interest in skateboarding and subsequently create a new subculture. The three friends, known as the Z-Boys, are credited with developing a new style of skateboarding in the mid-1970s that transformed the sport and became a worldwide phenomenon. Ferrera played "Thunder Monkey," a skating groupie and the girlfriend of Sid, one of the skaters' close friends. Her perfor-

Ferrera was thrilled to win the Golden Globe Award for Best Performance by an Actress in a TV Series.

mance has been cited by critics as one of the film's highlights. She also appeared in the family drama *How the Garcia Girls Spent Their Summer*, which was screened at the 2005 Sundance Film Festival. In this film, which explores the lives of three generations of Mexican-American women, Ferrera played Blanca, a 17-year-old on the verge of womanhood. Fed up with the boys in her neighborhood on the Arizona border, Blanca finds romance with an older boy from another town.

Ferrera then starred in the short film *3:52*, which won the Audience Award at the 2006 San Diego Women Film Festival, and the 2006 feature *Steel City*, which garnered nominations at the Independent Spirit Awards and the Sundance Film Festival. In 2007 she starred in the film *La Misma luna*, directed by Patricia Riggen. She also appeared as Sally in the off-Broadway production *Dog Sees God: Confessions of a Teenage Blockhead*, a take-off on the Charles Schulz comic strip *Peanuts*.

Recently, Ferrera starred in and executive produced the crime thriller *Towards Darkness*, which premiered at the Tribeca Film Festival in May 2007. Written and directed by José Antonio Negret, *Towards Darkness* is a Spanish-language drama concerning kidnapping in Columbia. The movie is based on Negret's 2004 short film *Darkness Minus Twelve*, in which Ferrera was also featured. Notably, the picture is the first in which she acts entirely in Spanish, which she found nerve-wracking. "I practiced with a dialogue coach . . . I knew that I could fool people who didn't speak Spanish, but a Spanish-speaking audience, I'm afraid they might know [that I'm not a native speaker]." She plans to film the sequel to *Sisterhood of the Traveling Pants* in summer 2007 before beginning work on season two of "Ugly Betty."

Being a Role Model

Ferrera's work has been praised for representing men and women of Latin American descent in a realistic and positive light. For example, California Representative Hilda L. Solis addressed her accomplishments on the floor of Congress, stating: "Through her work, Ms. Ferrera is breaking down barriers for Latinos in prime-time television." Ferrera has frequently commented on the response that she has gotten from her fans. "Just last weekend, I read a letter from a young girl. I did the cover of *CosmoGIRL!*, and she was thanking the magazine for putting me on the cover, because, 'When I watched "Ugly Betty," it was the first time in my life that I felt beautiful.' That was overwhelming for me. All you can ever hope to do in this business is touch one person, and yet I'm sure there were others."

> "Anyone who's ever felt like an outsider can see themselves in [Betty] and feel represented. And who hasn't, at some point in their life, felt like they didn't belong?"

Ferrera has received attention in the media for her healthy body image and the positive example she sets for young women about the issue of weight and physical appearance: "I don't think your jean size is what makes you a person. It's about the persistence inside of you, and you want tons of that with you at all times. . . . Caring about your appearance is universal. I know 45-year-old women who still hate their bodies. There are no magazines that say 'love who you are on the inside first, and worry about the outside later.'"

Ferrera's character on "Ugly Betty" has been embraced as a role model by a number of different groups, including adolescent girls, the gay community, Latinas, and the fashion crowd. Remarking on the character's universal appeal, she stated: "Anyone who's ever felt like an outsider can see themselves in her and feel represented. And who hasn't, at some point in their life, felt like they didn't belong?" Although being a role model can be a heavy responsibility for a young actress, she has remained positive. "I don't mind being the spokesperson for things as long as I believe in them."

HOME AND FAMILY

Ferrera lives in Los Angeles with her boyfriend, Ryan Piers Williams and their pet golden retriever, Buddy. Ferrera met him at the University of Southern California while working on his student film project. Williams is an aspiring filmmaker from Texas who currently works for director Steven Soderbergh. She has adamantly denied rumors that she is engaged to be married. "It's totally not true!" she has insisted. "And his mom called me and my sisters were calling me, and I was like, 'Are you kidding? Did you not think I would tell you first?'" Although she is not presently planning a wedding, she has stated that she wants a large family someday.

HOBBIES AND OTHER INTERESTS

Ferrera has taken time out from her busy schedule to support young independent filmmakers. She made an appearance at the 14th annual San Diego Latino Film Festival in early 2007 in support of *Muertas*, a short film by her boyfriend, Ryan Piers Williams. She spoke to the crowd at the festival, complimenting the filmmakers for their vision: "I think this event is a testament to what you can do. You find stories you believe in, and you do what you can to tell them," she said. She also served as an executive producer on the project, in which she has a brief cameo. "She really believes in the film and she's really supportive," Williams told the *San Diego Union-Tribune*.

Ferrera enjoys spending time with her family and loved ones, including her dog. She loves to dance and considers taking her mom to see "Dancing with the Stars" as one of the highlights of being a celebrity. She prefers to keep busy and finds enjoyment in her work: "When there's a film I want to do, sleep doesn't matter," she explained. "Part of me would love to be sitting in the sun in Italy, but I'd be crazy by day four." She admits that she struggles to control her natural drive for achievement. "The hardest part of this year has been learning to enjoy it. It's almost like a full-time job reminding myself to live in the moment and not look for more, more, more," she remarked. Still, she has learned an important lesson about finding contentment: "Happiness is something that you have to decide to have in your life," she said. "No amount of accolades can make you a happy person, and learning that as young as I did was a gift."

SELECTED CREDITS

Television

Gotta Kick It Up!, 2002 (movie)
Plainsong, 2004 (movie)
"Ugly Betty," 2006- (series)

Films

Real Women Have Curves, 2002
The Sisterhood of the Traveling Pants, 2005
Lords of Dogtown, 2005
How the Garcia Girls Spent Their Summer, 2005
Steel City, 2006
La Misma luna, 2007
Towards Darkness, 2007 (also executive producer)

HONORS AND AWARDS

Special Jury Prize for Acting (Sundance Film Festival): 2002, for *Real Women Have Curves* (with Lupe Ontiveros)
The Actor Award (Screen Actors Guild): 2007, Outstanding Performance by a Female Actor in a Comedy Series, for "Ugly Betty"
Golden Globe Award (Hollywood Foreign Press Association): 2007, Best Performance by an Actress in a Television Series—Musical or Comedy, for "Ugly Betty"
The *Time* 100—The People Who Shape Our World: 2007

FURTHER READING

Periodicals

America, Feb. 12, 2007, p.18
CosmoGIRL!, Feb. 2007, p.84
Entertainment Weekly, Sep. 8, 2006, p.108; Mar. 16, 2007, p.28
Los Angeles Times, May 8, 2005, p.E4; Sep. 17, 2006, p.8E; Nov. 8, 2006, p.E1; Jan. 29, 2007, p.E1
People, Oct. 2, 2006, p.146; Feb. 5, 2007, p.132
Teen People, Sep. 1, 2002, p.160
USA Today, Oct. 18, 2002, p.E2; Nov. 16, 2006, p.D1
Variety, Sep. 25, 2006, p.68

Online Articles

http://www.abcnews.go.com
  (*ABC News*, Good Morning America, "America Ferrera Makes 'Ugly'
  Beautiful," Jan. 8, 2007)
http://www.cosmogirl.com
  (*Cosmo Girl!*, "Miss America!," Feb. 2007)
http://www.ew.com
  (*Entertainment Weekly*, "America's Journey," May 8, 2007)
http://www.splicedonline.com
  (*SPLICEDwire: Film Reviews, News & Interviews*, "All American Girl,"
  Sep. 18, 2002)
http://www.style.com
  (*W Magazine*, "Hot Betty," May 2007)
http://www.time.com
  (*Time*, "The Time 100: America Ferrera," undated)
http://www.variety.com
  (*Variety*, "10 Actors to Watch: TV Class," Sep. 28, 2006)

ADDRESS

America Ferrera
"Ugly Betty"
ABC TV
77 West 66th Street
New York, NY 10023

WORLD WIDE WEB SITE

http://abc.go.com/primetime/uglybetty

Wendy Kopp 1967-

American Education Activist
President and Founder of Teach for America

BIRTH

Wendy Kopp was born in Austin, Texas, on June 29, 1967. Her parents, Jay D. and Mary Pat Kopp, were the owners of a company called Convention Guides, Inc., which published guidebooks for travelers. She has a brother, David, who is two years younger.

YOUTH

Kopp was raised near Dallas, Texas, in the wealthy suburb of University Park. She went to Highland Park High School, a public school near her home, and graduated in 1985.

Kopp was always a high achiever. She was editor of the student newspaper, took part in theater productions, and was a member of the debate team. She was also her class valedictorian, the student with the highest grade point average in her graduating class. In addition, she had a part-time job at a crafts store and helped out at her parents' business. She and her friends liked to go for long walks and have "very intense, very engaging conversations about big, abstract issues like 'Does God Exist?'" remembered Neeta Vallab, one of her friends from the debate team. "I think we probably thought of ourselves as the cooler smart kids."

EDUCATION

After graduating from high school, Kopp went to Princeton University in Princeton, New Jersey. There, she majored in public policy, the study of how public authorities can deal with society's problems. Her roommate during her freshman year was a woman from the South Bronx in New York City. She came from a low-income area where most families are poor and schools struggle with intractable social and economic problems. Kopp saw that her roommate was "absolutely brilliant," yet she struggled to keep up with her basic coursework because her school had not prepared her for college.

> *Kopp and her friends liked to go for long walks and have "very intense, very engaging conversations about big, abstract issues like 'Does God Exist?'" remembered Neeta Vallab, a friend from the debate team. "I think we probably thought of ourselves as the cooler smart kids."*

In theory, public education is supposed to give all American citizens an equal opportunity to achieve. But in reality, Kopp soon learned, being born in an affluent area with good schools gives a person a much better chance to excel than being born in an under-funded area with struggling schools. Many studies have documented this. For example, one study showed that children who live in low-income neighborhoods are seven times less likely to earn a college degree than those from wealthier neighborhoods. Nine-year-old children in low-income schools are, on average, three to four reading levels behind nine-year-olds who attend schools in higher-income districts.

Teach for America participant Joseph Leslie-Bernard helps his students work through math problems at a school in the Bronx in New York City.

Hard Work Brings Success

At Princeton, Kopp kept up the busy pace she had set for herself in high school. She worked for the Foundation for Student Communication (FSC), an organization that runs a yearly conference where students and business leaders meet. The foundation also publishes the magazine *Business Today*. Kopp got started with the FSC doing some writing for *Business Today*, and within two months, she was the publication's associate editor. Issues of *Business Today* usually had 32 pages, and the magazine's yearly revenue was about $300,000. This was not considered successful. "We couldn't sell ads and couldn't publish some issues," Kopp recalled. "There was a whole group of us who really worked to turn things around. We totally did. It became a complete obsession. We built it up to the point where it made $1.4 million. At one point, we put out a 140-page magazine."

That increased success didn't come easily. Kopp often worked 70 hours per week at the FSC, but her dedication paid off. She was president of the organization during her senior year at Princeton. By that time, she was managing a budget of $1.5 million dollars, nearly five times as much as the annual budget had been when she first became involved with the FSC.

An Ambitious Senior Project

During the fall of her senior term, Kopp organized an FSC conference about education reform. One of the topics covered there was the critical shortage of qualified teachers in low-income communities. There are many reasons for this problem, but Kopp felt that one of them is the image of teaching as a profession. Top graduates from the best schools are aggressively recruited to work for banking and investment firms, as well as other corporations, and the financial rewards for employment with those companies can be great. Teachers, on the other hand, are not recruited in the same way, and teaching is not viewed as a profession with high potential for career advancement. Kopp began to think about how this problem could be addressed.

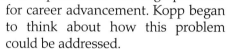

"My generation was dubbed the 'Me Generation.' People thought all we wanted to do was focus on ourselves and make a lot of money. But that didn't strike me as right. I felt as if thousands of us talented, driven graduating seniors were searching for a way to make a social impact."

Then an idea came to her: Why not have a national teacher corps that would aggressively recruit top graduates, just as the banking and investment firms do? Inspired by the thought, she wrote a letter about it to George H.W. Bush, who was then president of the United States. In response, she received a standard job-rejection letter. Undaunted, Kopp began to outline her idea as part of her senior project at Princeton. She called her thesis "A Plan and Argument for the Creation of a National Teacher Corps." In it, she proposed starting up a nonprofit organization that would recruit the top college students in America, give them eight weeks of intensive training, and place them in six of the nation's most troubled school districts for a period of two years. She proposed doing this with a budget of $2.5 million, to be funded through donations from big businesses and foundations.

Kopp's idea was very ambitious. She wanted not just to bring additional teachers into the schools for short-term help, but also to fundamentally change the school system and the image of teaching. She knew top students were very competitive about getting into public service programs—in part because service in the Peace Corps and other programs looks great on a resume when looking for another job. She wanted her teacher corps to have the same kind of selective, high-minded image.

"We're not going to have a first-class education system as long as the public views teaching as downwardly mobile," Kopp reasoned. "We want to try to change that, to show the public that outstanding individuals compete to enter this profession and that they find it incredibly challenging and rewarding." She also believed that people who had worked for a national teacher corps would feel inspired to keep trying to improve the quality of American education, even long after they finished their service with the corps. If she were able to recruit high-achieving students, they would probably continue to lend their involvement and financial support after they went on to take over important positions in business and government.

Kopp's advisor considered her plan noble, but unrealistic. Knowing how hard it can be to raise even a few thousand dollars, he suggested starting with just 50 teachers and working in one test location. But Kopp refused to alter her plan: she believed that if she downscaled her operation, it would never really work. Full of enthusiasm, she revised her senior thesis into a working business proposal. In 1989, Kopp graduated from Princeton with her Bachelor of Arts (BA) degree in public policy. She had applied for jobs at several top business firms, but she failed to get any of those positions. So she got to work making her senior thesis a reality.

CAREER HIGHLIGHTS

Kopp faced significant challenges in implementing her idea. Many people doubted that she would be able to get students to sign on. After all, their pay would be minimal, and they would have to go into some depressed, troubled areas to tackle tough, long-standing problems. "My generation was dubbed the 'Me Generation.' People thought all we wanted to do was focus on ourselves and make a lot of money," Kopp later said. "But that didn't strike me as right. I felt as if thousands of us talented, driven graduating seniors were searching for a way to make a social impact but simply couldn't find the opportunity to do so." She felt if she could make her idea a reality, "it would make a huge difference in kids' lives, and that ultimately it could change the very consciousness of our country, by influencing the thinking and career paths of a generation of leaders."

Kopp wanted to "surround teaching with many of the same factors surrounding investment banking and management consulting: Create an aura of service and status and selectivity. Recruit college students aggressively. Make teaching accessible to people who did not major in education. And make it a two-year commitment, on the theory that the experience will shape their interests and that a lot of them will continue in education."

*Megan Nix helps her students with an in-class
English assignment at a school in New Orleans.*

The teaching recruits wouldn't only be drawn from the ranks of education majors, but from all fields. They would be people who had demonstrated strong leadership qualities. Kopp believed that these energetic people would bring inspiration and new ideas to depressed areas. She hoped that their example would inspire their students to work for positive change in their own lives and in their communities, too.

Founding Teach for America

Kopp decided to call her teacher corps Teach for America. After writing her business plan, her next job was to raise enough start-up money. She has described herself as shy, but she had learned how to communicate effectively with business leaders during her time with the FCS. The need for funds for Teach for America (TFA) gave her the courage to start phoning every major business and foundation she could think of to solicit funds. She sent her proposal and a request for funding to the chief executive officers of 30 major corporations.

In June 1989, the month that she graduated from Princeton, she received her first response, a letter from the Mobil Corporation offering her $26,000 to help get TFA started. She used that money to travel, meeting with representatives from various school districts and corporations. At the same time, she and her team were recruiting students at many of the best colleges in the country, using such simple methods as sliding flyers about the program under doorways in dormitories.

One year after her graduation, Kopp had the $2.5 million she had envisioned in her plan. In addition to the first donation from Mobil, she had obtained funds from the Chrysler Corporation, the pharmaceutical giant Merck, and other large companies. Union Carbide, another major corporation, had donated the use of office space in New York City. Texas billionaire Ross Perot had agreed to provide matching funds with the first $500,000 Kopp collected. In addition to funding, she had applications from 2,600 undergraduate students who wanted to join the TFA program.

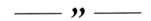

Kopp has said that her lack of experience helped her to achieve her goals. "My very greatest asset in reaching this point was that I simply did not understand what was impossible. I would soon learn the value of experience, but Teach for America would not exist today were it not for my naivete," she remarked. She believed something similar happens with the students and teachers in her program: "I see this same phenomenon every day as I watch 23-year-olds walking into classrooms and setting

Reflecting on TFA's first year, Kopp said, "There were many times when I wasn't sure I was going to make it. There was a lot of failure and there were many mistakes, just as there were successes."

goals for themselves and their students that most people believe to be entirely unrealistic." Like Kopp, many of those teachers and students go on to meet or exceed their own lofty goals.

A Strong Start

In fall 1990, after attending their intensive training workshops, the first TFA recruits went into schools in some of the poorest areas in the United States. Their destinations included such urban locations as New Orleans, Houston, Los Angeles, and New York City, as well as rural areas in the South and Southwest. TFA recruits went into public schools, where teachers are required to meet certain standards. These vary by state but virtually all include a college degree in education or a related field plus certification by the state. But TFA recruits came from all fields of study and did not necessarily have any college credits in the field of education. Since the schools in which they taught were already experiencing serious teacher shortages, these schools were allowed to hire substitutes who had no teaching credentials or experience.

In that first year, there were a lot of challenges to meet and lessons to learn. Some studies say that it takes at least two years of classroom experience to become an effective teacher. Kopp and her staff learned firsthand that it was difficult to train people and equip them to go into the classroom in just eight weeks. Added to that difficulty was the fact that many of the students in the schools served by TFA struggled with hunger, drugs, and crime in their daily lives.

Not all educators supported TFA. In fact, recruits sometimes faced resentment from long-term teachers. Some teachers believed these inexperienced newcomers lacked the knowledge and skill to handle a tough classroom. They also worried the TFA recruits came to shake things up, only to leave two years later. Some recruits couldn't handle the cultural differences they faced in the communities where they had been assigned and left their positions, but most of them stuck it out. Many went on to see their students meet and even exceed the goals they had set, dramatically improving their test scores, working many extra hours in the classroom, and becoming strong learners. Reflecting on TFA's first year, Kopp said, "There were many times when I wasn't sure I was going to make it. There was a lot of failure and there were many mistakes, just as there were successes."

Criticism, Setbacks, and Recovery

By 1992, TFA had 1,200 teachers at work and had raised more than $12 million. But just two years later, the foundation suffered a serious setback. Linda Darling-Hammond, a highly respected professor of education and co-director of the National Center for Restructuring Education, Schools, and Teaching, published a lengthy article titled, "Who Will Speak for the Children? How 'Teach for America' Hurts Urban Schools and Students." Darling-Hammond argued that TFA encouraged an overly simple approach to teaching, created staffing disruptions and morale problems in the schools where the program was allowed, and produced ineffective teachers. She concluded that TFA was bad both for children and for the teaching profession.

Kopp countered those claims by pointing out a report in which more than 90 percent of school principals who had hired TFA teachers said they considered them an asset to their schools, gave them very favorable evaluations, and felt they would definitely hire from TFA again. She also showed that about 60 percent of TFA alumni remain involved with education in some way after their term of service was up, and almost all of them report that working for the foundation gave them a strong sense of social responsibility.

TFA had also been criticized as "elitist" for sending many white teachers into minority neighborhoods, but Kopp argued that TFA had a much higher percentage of minority teachers than the teaching profession as a whole. As for charges that TFA teachers were unfairly bypassing normal requirements for certification, Kopp argued that the schools that hired them were already forced to hire unaccredited individuals as teachers because there were no qualified applicants. TFA's defenders also stressed that Darling-Hammond strongly defended the existing system. But that system included many students who were failing, which demonstrated that there were many ongoing, serious problems that she failed to address.

Even though Kopp disputed her critics, some key supporters of TFA chose to withdraw their funding following the publication of Darling-Hammond's article. Faced with having to shut TFA down completely due to lack of money, Kopp personally phoned all her contacts to ask for emergency donations to keep the foundation afloat. She managed to avoid a complete shutdown, but by 1996, she had been forced to slash TFA's budget almost in half in order to survive. She also had to cut 60 jobs from the staff.

"Your idealism can enable you to pursue noble aims, but it takes hard work and personal growth and a kind of determined patience to see them actually come to be."

By 2000, things seemed to be looking up. Don Fisher, the founder of the Gap chain of clothing stores, offered TFA an $8.3 million challenge grant that year. If Kopp could raise that much from other sources, he would match the amount. Within four months, TFA had raised $25 million. Furthermore, U.S. President George W. Bush seemed to take a strong interest in TFA. He met with its staff, mentioned it in speeches as an example of an admirable service organization, and designated it as a program that would get special attention from First Lady Laura Bush. Later, however, TFA learned that the promised support from the government had been cut.

A Leader with Vision

In good times and bad, Kopp has remained a strong leader, willing to work hard to make her ideas become reality. After sleeping just four or five

*Sen. Edward Kennedy giving Kopp the John F. Kennedy
New Frontier Award for her commitment to public service.*

hours a night, she gets up at about 3:00 or 4:00 in the morning, spends a little time on her computer, then goes for a five-mile run. Then she is ready to start her 15-hour workday. Kopp is not known as a "people person," but she is a hard worker and good organizer. She has shown confidence in her own way of doing things. During TFA's low point, some of the staff threatened to quit if she didn't start making her decisions more democratically. She didn't agree to their demands, but no one quit.

In 2001, Kopp published a memoir about her experiences with TFA titled *One Day, All Children...: The Unlikely Triumph of Teach for America and What I Learned Along the Way*. The book was recommended by a reviewer for *Publishers Weekly*: "Kopp has brought a fresh approach to the educational process that has proved effective; her inspiring story will challenge schools and professional educators to take notice, while motivating college seniors and recent graduates to join her team."

Some critics have questioned Kopp's lack of background in education. But she has argued that she is not trying to use TFA as a means to fix all the problems within the American educational system. Instead, she is trying to build up interest in educational issues and to encourage fresh thinking. She has described the foundation as a social-justice organization, not a model for teacher training. "We don't feel that we have the answers at all. The challenge is to remember that there's always a better way. That's the responsibility of the leaders of an organization," she said. As for her own qualifications, she admitted, "I think Teach for America has suffered from the fact that I did not teach, in a major way." But she also said that "I also think if I had taught, I wouldn't have started Teach for America."

Kopp has realized her dream of recruiting talented college students just as well as any investment firm or large corporation. TFA is now one of the largest hirers of college seniors. In 2006, 19,000 college seniors applied to TFA, including a full 10 percent of the graduating class of Yale University. Of those 19,000 applicants, only one in eight will be asked to join the corps. That year, her organization had a budget of $70 million and could claim that it had served 2.5 million students in 1,000 schools, located in 25 different communities. In 2006, the New York City public schools hired 8 percent of their new teachers from TFA, and in Newark, New Jersey, about 30 percent of new teachers were hired from TFA.

Over the years, Kopp has won a variety of awards for her service to TFA, including the 2003 Clinton Center Award for Leadership and National Service from the Democratic Leadership Council, the 2003 Outstanding Social Entrepreneur Award from the Schwab Foundation, and the 2004 John F. Kennedy New Frontier Award from the John F. Kennedy Library Foundation and the Institute of Politics at the Kennedy School of Government, Harvard University. In 2006, Kopp's achievements were recognized with the Austin College Leadership Award. She was chosen over several other contenders, including U2's Bono, television journalist Bill Moyers, and New Mexico governor Bill Richardson. The honor included a $100,000 prize, which she donated directly to TFA.

Looking back on all the roadblocks TFA has had to overcome, Kopp said, "Luckily, I don't worry all that much. . . . I really have this attitude that things will work out. All those little obstacles that people think will stop everything—you can get around anything." She doesn't pretend that success can come merely through positive thinking, however. "Your idealism can enable you to pursue noble aims, but it takes hard work and personal growth and a kind of determined patience to see them actually come to be."

MARRIAGE AND FAMILY

Wendy Kopp married Richard Barth Jr. in New York City on February 7, 1998. Barth is a former TFA staff member and is the chief executive officer of the Knowledge is Power Program (KIPP), another organization dedicated to improving the quality of America's schools. They live in New York City with their three sons, Benjamin, Francis, and Haddon.

HOBBIES AND OTHER INTERESTS

In 1997, Kopp also founded the New Teacher Project, an organization that works in a variety of ways to improve teacher quality and to recruit new, high-quality teachers into high-need schools. Rather than drawing from the pool of recent college graduates, the New Teacher Project recruits professionals who are in the middle of their careers. She has remained on the Board of Directors of this organization and is also on the board of the Learning Project, another association that seeks to launch and maintain quality schools for children in high-need areas. She has also served on advisory boards of the Center for Public Leadership at Harvard University's Kennedy School of Government, and the National Council on Teacher Quality.

WRITINGS

One Day, All Children...: The Unlikely Triumph of Teach for America and What I Learned along the Way, 2001

HONORS AND AWARDS

Voice of Conscience Award (Aetna Foundation): 1994
Citizen Activist Award (Gleitsman Foundation): 1994
Clinton Center Award for Leadership and National Service (Democratic Leadership Council): 2003
Outstanding Social Entrepreneur Award (Schwab Foundation): 2003
John F. Kennedy New Frontier Award (John F. Kennedy Library Foundation and the Institute of Politics at the Kennedy School of Government, Harvard University): 2004
Austin College Leadership Award: 2006

FURTHER READING

Books

Kopp, Wendy. *One Day, All Children...: The Unlikely Triumph of Teach for America and What I Learned along the Way*, 2001

Periodicals

Christian Science Monitor, Mar. 20, 2001, p.3
Current Biography Yearbook, 2003
Forbes, Oct. 14, 1991, p.S22
Fortune, Nov. 27, 2006, p.87
New York Times, June 20, 1990, p.A1; Jan. 7, 1996, Education Life Supplement, sec.4A, p.26; Nov. 12, 2000, Education Life Supplement, sec.4A, p.23
People, May 28, 2001, p.131
Time, Aug. 25, 2004, p.23

Online Articles

http://www.unc.edu
    (University of North Carolina at Chapel Hill, transcript of commencement address given by Wendy Kopp, May 14, 2006)

ADDRESS

Wendy Kopp
Teach for America
315 West 36th Street
7th Floor
New York, NY 10018

WORLD WIDE WEB SITE

http://www.teachforamerica.com

Nancy Pelosi 1940-

American Political Leader
First Woman to Serve as Speaker of the United
States House of Representatives

BIRTH

Nancy Pelosi was born Nancy Patricia D'Alesandro on March
26, 1940, in Baltimore, Maryland. Her father was Thomas
D'Alesandro Jr. and her mother was Annunciata "Nancy"
Lombardi D'Alesandro. The youngest of six children, Pelosi
has five older brothers: Thomas III, Nicholas, Hector, Joseph,
and Franklin.

Pelosi's father served as the mayor of Baltimore from 1947-1959, beginning when she was seven years old. A born political leader, D'Alesandro had previously held seats in the Maryland legislature, the Baltimore City Council, and the United States Congress. Nancy's mother helped her husband in his political aspirations. A member of the Democratic Women's Club, her mother dropped out of law school to focus on her family. "My father was more the centerpiece," explained Pelosi's oldest brother, Thomas III. "We all rallied around him and his career, and none rallied more than my mother. But as successful as my father was, we all knew my mother was the strength of the family."

YOUTH

Pelosi's family lived on Albemarle Street in the Little Italy section of Baltimore. Like most of the children in her Italian-American neighborhood, "Little Nancy" spent time playing on the front stoops of the row houses on her block and visiting the local candy store.

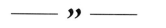

"Our whole lives were politics," Pelosi said about her childhood. "If you entered the house, it was always campaign time, and if you went into the living room, it was always constituent time."

The Pelosi family's three-story brick home was used as her father's political headquarters, and city residents frequently visited their home to voice complaints or discuss issues of concern. "People would come to the door and they wanted help," she remembered. "My father always knew how to refer to people. And they'd end up having dinner at our house, because they were hungry." She sometimes sat behind a desk at the front door, greeting visitors and directing them to various city departments. "Our whole lives were politics," she explained. "If you entered the house, it was always campaign time, and if you went into the living room, it was always constituent time." Being the mayor's daughter had its perks. In 1957, she accompanied her father to a formal dinner where she was seated next to future U.S president John F. Kennedy.

Her father and the Democratic leaders of his time helped inform Pelosi's growing political awareness. "It was always about the progressive economic agenda for a fair economy, where many Americans, all Americans, could participate in the economic success of our country," she said. Faith was also an important component of the D'Alesandro

Pelosi as a young girl with her family.

household. "I was raised . . . in a very strict upbringing in a Catholic home where we respected people, were observant, [and where] the fundamental belief was that God gave us all a free will and we were accountable for that, each of us," she explained. "We were all christened into the Roman Catholic Church and the Democratic Party." Overall, these experiences growing up prepared her for the future. According to Representative Anna G. Eshoo, "Nancy's life was a dress rehearsal for what she's doing now."

EDUCATION

Pelosi attended St. Leo's Catholic school, a few blocks from her house. When her father was elected mayor, he received a car and driver, and seven-year-old Nancy began to be chauffeured to school, though she insisted on walking the last block to avoid embarrassment. After graduating from the Institute of Notre Dame, an all-girls Catholic high school, she attended Trinity College, a small women's college in Washington DC. She graduated in 1962 with a Bachelor of Arts (BA) degree in political science.

MARRIAGE AND FAMILY

Pelosi met her husband, Paul, while she was attending Trinity College and he was enrolled at nearby Georgetown University. They married in 1963, shortly after she graduated from college. They soon moved to New York City, where Paul pursued a career as an investment banker. In 1969, the couple settled in his hometown, San Francisco. While she stayed home to raise their five children—Nancy Corinne, Christine, Jacqueline, Paul, and Alexandra—her husband became a successful businessman in the fields of computer technology and real estate.

For Pelosi, being a stay-at-home mom was a full-time job. "When you raise five children born six years apart, you do most of the work yourself. You can't attract a good deal of people to help out," she joked. Being a devoted mother taught her skills that would later help her in her political career. "It trains you to anticipate, to be organized, and to be flexible," she noted. "To me, the center of my life will always be raising my family. It is the complete joy of my life. To me, working in Congress is a continuation of that."

> "[Being a mother] trains you to anticipate, to be organized, and to be flexible," Pelosi noted. "To me, the center of my life will always be raising my family. It is the complete joy of my life. To me, working in Congress is a continuation of that."

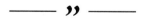

FIRST JOBS

While raising a family in San Francisco, Pelosi did volunteer work during the early 1970s for the city's Democratic Party. Some of those efforts were to support the governor of California, Jerry Brown, who was also a childhood friend of Paul Pelosi. Brown soon became involved in national politics as well.

In 1976 the Democrats were looking for a strong candidate to run for president against the Republican incumbent, President Gerald Ford. Jimmy Carter, the former governor of Georgia, seemed to be the Democratic favorite. Despite Carter's lead, Jerry Brown decided to enter the presidential race and compete in the Maryland primary. Primary elections are held throughout the country by both the Democratic and Republican parties; they are used to determine who will become the Democratic and the Republican candidates in the presidential election. Brown wanted to beat Carter for the Democratic candidacy. Brown recruited Pelosi to help him in

Pelosi at the headquarters of her first
congressional campaign on the night of the election, 1987.

the race because she still had strong family and political ties to Maryland. Against all odds, Brown managed to get more votes than Carter in Maryland, although Carter would eventually win both the Democratic candidacy and the presidential election. But Pelosi's invaluable help with this small victory did not go unnoticed. She was soon elected chair of the Northern California branch of the Democratic Party, subsequently becoming the head of the party for the entire state.

After the election, Pelosi continued raising her children and volunteering in Democratic politics. Her efforts were soon rewarded. San Francisco Congresswoman Sala Burton became ill with cancer in 1987, and she chose Pelosi to run for her seat in the U.S. Congress in the upcoming election. Though Pelosi had always put her children before her political aspirations, she decided that they were now old enough that she could give up her duties as a full-time mother.

Pelosi's opponent was Harry Britt, a San Francisco City Supervisor who was openly gay, which made him very popular among the members of San

Francisco's large homosexual community. She relied on the fundraising skills that she learned during the Brown campaign and accumulated one million dollars in less than two months. In the end, she defeated Britt by a small margin. Fred Ross Jr., who helped organize her campaign, attested to her political skills. "She has an organizer's instinct. An organizer has to have imagination, has to have a very strategic mind about how to think about a campaign, how to organize a campaign and how to win it. What are the vulnerabilities of the other side? What are the resources you can amass? She understands all of that."

CAREER HIGHLIGHTS

Since 1987, Pelosi has been a member of the United States House of Representatives. During this time, she has become well known as a champion of liberal causes. She has been active in the areas of human rights, particularly in China, as well as gay and lesbian rights. She has worked for gun control and sponsored the Brady Bill, which called for background checks for persons attempting to buy guns. This bill was signed into law in 1993. Additionally, she has been a vocal opponent of the federal death penalty, has rejected proposals to drill for oil in Alaska, and has advocated the legalization of medical marijuana.

> "I will fight discrimination of any form, including gays and lesbians," Pelosi emphasized. "If that makes me unacceptable to some people, that is very fundamental to me and everyone should know it from the start."

Pelosi also strongly endorsed the Challenge America program, a branch of the National Endowment for the Arts (NEA) designed to fund the arts in small towns and urban areas. In 2001 her support paid off when Congress voted to fund the program. On the floor of the House of Representatives, she claimed that "today's vote by the House to increase funding for the NEA . . . is a victory of imagination over ideology. In recent years, we have worried a great deal about the digital divide—a lack of access to technology that could limit opportunity to lower-income Americans. We should be equally concerned about a creativity crisis."

Criticism of the Chinese Government

Pelosi has paid special attention to issues related to the Chinese government and their approach to human rights. One contributing factor occurred in

1989. Approximately 100,000 Chinese students staged a protest in Beijing's Tiananmen Square against their Communist government. The protest lasted for two months, until the military took deadly action against the students. Hundreds of protesters are thought to have been killed. In 1991, Pelosi was one of three members of Congress to travel to China. Along with her colleagues, she made a visit to Tiananmen Square during their trip. They held up a banner that read: "To those who died for democracy in China." As the press gathered to cover the event, the Chinese police closed in. "I started running," she recalled. "My colleagues, some of them got a little roughed up. The press got treated worse because they had cameras, and they were detained."

Throughout the 1990s, Pelosi protested the meetings between Chinese officials and members of the U.S. Congress. She opposed President Bill Clinton's 1998 diplomatic trip to China and decried the International Olympic Committee's decision to hold the 2008 Summer Olympic Games in China. To this day, she keeps a picture of herself holding up the banner in Tiananmen Square and continues to speak out against the oppression of the Chinese people by their government.

AIDS and Gay Rights

AIDS and gay rights are also significant issues for Pelosi. During her time in Congress, she has supported funding for research into the AIDS epidemic. Because of the large population of gay men afflicted with AIDS in and around San Francisco, this issue is close to her heart. Prior to her arrival in the House of Representatives, the U.S. government had taken no significant action toward dealing with AIDS. Once elected, she became involved in the creation of the Housing Opportunities for Persons with AIDS program. This initiative supplies federal housing aid to victims of the disease and their families. She also backed legislation that extends Medicaid (a federal program that helps pay medical bills) to men and women with AIDS.

Pelosi's work for gay rights has been widely recognized in the gay community. According to *The Advocate*, a national gay and lesbian magazine, "[Pelosi] is considered one of the House's staunchest supporters of gay rights and a leader on AIDS issues since she arrived on Capitol Hill in 1987." Furthermore, Pelosi has pushed for the legalization of same-sex marriages and promoted the rights of gay couples to adopt children in Washington DC. She remains steadfast in her dedication to issues of gay rights. "I will fight discrimination of any form, including gays and lesbians," she emphasized. "If that makes me unacceptable to some people, that is very fundamental to me and everyone should know it from the start."

Congresswoman Pelosi on the floor of the U.S. House with her grandchildren.

Becoming the Democratic Whip

In 1999 Pelosi began campaigning for the position of Democratic whip, a leadership position in the U.S. House of Representatives. The leadership roles in the House of Representatives are tied to the status of the major parties. Many important benefits are tied to being the majority party, the party with the most members in the House. And with elections for the House of Representatives held every two years, the majority and minority parties can switch frequently.

The House of Representatives is led by the speaker of the house, who is elected by the majority party. The next level of leadership is the party leader—one for each party—who is referred to as the majority leader or the minority leader. Below that is the whip, the position Pelosi was seeking. The job of the whip—the majority and minority whip, one for each party—is to make sure that the members of his or her party are working together as a group and are voting along the same lines.

Beginning in 1994, the Democrats became the minority party in the House of Representatives. At that time, Democrat Bill Clinton was president, and

Al Gore was vice president. The Democrats were expecting Clinton to win a second term as president in the 1996 election, and they expected Al Gore to win the presidential election in 2000. Democrats also assumed that if the voters were going to elect a Democrat president, then the voters would also elect more Democrats to the House of Representatives. In that case, the Democrats would become the majority party. If that were to happen, then Democrat Richard A. Gephardt, who was then the House minority leader, would become the speaker of the house. This would allow the Democratic whip to become the new majority leader. Pelosi saw this as an excellent opportunity to advance in the ranks of the Democratic leadership, and she started campaigning early for the position of minority whip.

The presidential election of 2000 turned out to be far more complicated than anyone expected. Al Gore lost the election to George W. Bush after a lengthy legal dispute involving the counting of ballots in Florida. Similarly, the Democrats failed to secure enough new seats to become the majority party in the House. Despite the blow to her party, Pelosi successfully defeated fellow Democratic Representative Steny Hoyer for the position of minority whip in 2001. This victory made her the first woman in United States history to hold the position of whip in the House of Representatives.

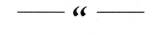

According to her brother, Thomas III, "The day Nancy was sworn in [as Democratic whip] was one of the happiest days of my mother's life. [Nancy] was the reincarnation of my mother's ambition."

"I think there was a glass ceiling for women in politics," Pelosi stated. "I think I did break that. I think my election as House Democratic whip sent a very clear message. . . . It took some getting used to for people to think that I will now move into the Capitol with my offices there, to have the additional staff and opportunity that a woman hasn't had before in the House or in the Senate. And that I will have influence over how our party goes forward and hopefully on public policy. My candidacy was not about me. It was about showcasing the tremendous talent in the Democratic Party." Even Tom DeLay, the Republican majority whip, praised her victory. "She's a worthy opponent," he admitted. "I've always sort of liked her. But, obviously, I want to beat her at every turn."

While Pelosi was pleased with her new position, she couldn't help but notice that women still had many obstacles to overcome in Washington DC.

*As the head Democrat on the House Intelligence Committee,
Pelosi was deeply involved in hearings on the terririst attacks of 9/11.
Here she is shown with Rep. Jan Harman and Rep. James Clyburn.*

"Shortly after my election, the top congressional leaders were invited to the White House for a meeting with the president to talk about the agenda for the next session of Congress," she recounted. "I'd been there on many occasions, so I wasn't particularly apprehensive. But when the door closed behind us, I saw that there were very few other people at the table with the president, and of course they were all men. It occurred to me that this was unlike any meeting that I'd ever attended at the White House. In fact, because a woman was there as a top elected leader and not as staff, it was unlike any meeting ever held at the White House."

Pelosi's appointment as whip was a historic moment for women in the United States, and it resonated back home in Baltimore as well. According to her brother, Thomas III, "The day Nancy was sworn in was one of the happiest days of my mother's life. [Nancy] was the reincarnation of my mother's ambition."

Investigating 9/11

On September 11, 2001, terrorists hijacked four commercial airplanes in the United States and crashed them into the World Trade Center towers in New York City and the Pentagon in Washington DC; one plane crashed in a field in Pennsylvania. Almost 3,000 people died. The citizens of America were devastated and wondered what could have been done to prevent this horrifying incident. Congress created a House-Senate Joint Inquiry to investigate the events leading up to the terrorist attack.

As the head Democrat on the House Intelligence Committee, Pelosi played a large role in these hearings. In particular, the committee wanted to understand how the intelligence community (the FBI and CIA) processed the information that they had been gathering. "There was a report in August (2001) . . . [that said the terrorists] were planning a strike imminently in the U.S. but again, we didn't have a time and place. So we have to see where the breakdown was in the system," Pelosi stated. The committee was also interested in the lack of enforcement of immigration laws that allowed the hijackers into the county. "Was it a breakdown in communication with the Immigration and Naturalization Service," she asked. "I hope that we will have a review of all of the federal agencies which had a responsibility, which could have prevented what happened on September 11."

One agency that did not allow the committee access to all of its information was the National Security Council. The NSC consists of the president, vice president, secretary of state, and the foreign-policy experts who regularly meet with the president. Pelosi was angered by what she saw as a lack of cooperation. "If we're going to have a real and complete investigation, if we are going to get the job done for the families and for the country and protect the American people into the future, the National Security Council records must be available to the committee and the public," she asserted.

Although the Bush administration eventually provided some information to the National Commission on Terrorist Attacks in 2003, Pelosi argued that they were still protecting the government of Saudi Arabia. Many of the September 11 terrorists were from Saudi Arabia, but the Saudi government is one of the few American allies in the Middle East. The Bush administration explained that they were merely maintaining a diplomatic relationship with the Saudis and did not want to offend them. Pelosi countered by saying, "Classification should protect sources and methods, ongoing investigations, and our national security interests. It is not intended to protect reputations of people or countries."

Opposing the War in Iraq

A year after the terrorist attacks of September, 11, 2001, Congress was scheduled to vote on whether or not to endorse an invasion of Iraq. President George W. Bush insisted that the leader of Iraq, Saddam Hussein, was hiding weapons of mass destruction. During the 2001 State of the Union Address, President Bush asserted: "U.S. intelligence indicates that Saddam Hussein had upwards of 30,000 munitions capable of delivering chemical agents. Inspectors recently turned up 16 of them, despite Iraq's recent declaration denying their existence. Saddam Hussein has not accounted for the remaining 29,984 of these prohibited munitions. He has given no evidence that he has destroyed them." Republican whip Tom DeLay added, "Saddam Hussein is seeking the means to murder millions in just a single moment. He's trying to extend that grip of fear beyond his own borders and he is consumed with hatred for America." Consequently, many Democrats, including House minority leader Gephardt and Senate majority leader Tom Daschle, supported the use of military force against Iraq. "I believe it is important for America to speak with one voice," Daschle said at the time.

> "Becoming the first woman speaker will send a message to young girls and women across the country that anything is possible for them, that women can achieve power, wield power, and breathe the air at that altitude. As the first woman speaker of the House, I will work to make certain that I will not be the last."

This made it all the more uncomfortable for Pelosi to speak out against the war. During the debate leading up to the vote, she claimed that military conflict with Iraq "poses a risk to the war on terrorism. It will unravel the coalition [of Muslim allies in the Middle East]. It will make Arab countries that are friendly to our cause now shaky." Furthermore, her role as whip would normally force her to convince Democrats to vote along the same lines as their minority leader, Gephardt. But she insisted that the members of the House listen to their conscience. Although Congress eventually voted to back the war, less than half of the Democrats in the House of Representatives sided with Gephardt.

Shortly afterwards, the Republicans claimed even more seats in the House and Senate during the Congressional elections of 2002. The Democrats began to question Gephardt's leadership capabilities as House minority

Pelosi holds the speaker's gavel during opening day ceremonies, after being sworn in as the first female speaker of the U.S. House.

leader. Sensing the discontent within his party, Gephardt resigned from his position. Pelosi was elected to take his place, making her the first woman to hold the position of minority leader in Congress. "It was a very powerful vote of confidence," she acknowledged. "It was quite stunning, I have to admit myself. What it says is a recognition of what I can do as a leader to take us to victory." This new position only strengthened her resolve to speak out against the Iraq war, and she has continued to be one of the leading voices of Congressional opposition on this front.

Becoming Speaker of the U.S. House of Representatives

When Pelosi became the Democratic minority leader, many Republicans hoped that her left wing, or liberal, stances would actually hurt her party.

When the president addresses the House and Senate, as in this scene from the 2007 State of the Union address, he is flanked by the vice president and the speaker of the house. Here, President George W. Bush is shown with Vice President Dick Cheney and Speaker of the House Nancy Pelosi.

"If she is true to her past and her district," claimed Ohio Representative Deborah Pryce, "the Democratic caucus will be far too liberal for the country." Others were not so sure, including Porter J. Goss, a Republican representative who worked with her on the 9/11 inquiry. "Does she have the ability to go beyond representing the left wing of her party? The answer is clearly yes," Goss said. "While it's true she does represent the left wing of the [Democratic] party, it's equally true that if you say that's all she's going to do, you would be underestimating her badly."

In the November 2006 Congressional election, the Democrats gained the majority of the seats in both the Senate and the House of Representatives. This victory for the Democrats gave them control of Congress for the first time in 12 years. It also allowed the Democrats to vote for a new speaker of the house. They elected Pelosi. This was especially significant because the speaker of the house is second in line (after the vice president) to the presidency.

Just as she had been the first female congressional leader, Pelosi was now the first female speaker of the house. "When my colleagues elect me as speaker on January 4, we will not just break through a glass ceiling, we will break through a marble ceiling," she proclaimed. "In more than 200 years of history, there was an established pecking order and I cut in line." She added, "Becoming the first woman speaker will send a message to young girls and women across the country that anything is possible for them, that women can achieve power, wield power, and breathe the air at that altitude. As the first woman speaker of the House, I will work to make certain that I will not be the last."

When Pelosi was sworn in as the speaker of the house in early 2007, she was accompanied by her six grandchildren. "For our daughters and granddaughters," she proclaimed during her speech on the floor of the House of Representatives, "today we have broken the marble ceiling." President Bush acknowledged the historical relevance of her new position during the State of the Union Address that took place soon afterward. The president announced, "Tonight I have the high privilege and distinct honor of my own as the first president to begin the State of the Union Message with these words: 'Madam Speaker.'"

The First 100 Hours and Beyond

As Pelosi settled in as the speaker of the house for the 110th session of Congress, she pledged to focus on six legislative initiatives during the first 100 hours. These goals, which the Democratic Party had developed during the 2006 campaign year, were dubbed the "Six for '06": "We will make America safer by implementing the recommendations of the 9/11 Commission [a bipartisan plan to handle the escalating violence in Iraq with diplomacy]. We will make our economy fairer by raising the minimum wage. We will promote stem cell research to offer hope to the millions of American families who suffer from devastating diseases. We will improve health care by requiring Medicare to negotiate for lower prescription drug prices. We will make college more affordable by cutting interest rates on student loans. We will take the first step toward achieving energy independence by repealing subsidies to Big Oil and investing the savings in renewable energy." Yet some Republicans were skeptical of this plan and doubted that many of these goals would be achieved.

Meanwhile, the war in Iraq continued to spark heated debate. In January 2007, President Bush announced his plan to deploy more than 20,000 additional troops to Iraq in an effort to stop the increasing bloodshed. Pelosi voiced her opposition to this plan on the floor of the House in February 2007. "Let us be clear on one fundamental principle: we all support the troops," she emphasized. "Four previous troop escalations have resulted in escalating levels of violence. In light of the facts, President Bush's escalation proposal will not make America safer, will not make our military stronger, and will not make the region more stable, and it will not have my support."

HOBBIES AND OTHER INTERESTS

Pelosi is a self-admitted chocoholic and has professed a particular weakness for chocolate mousse. Her favorite television show is "The Daily Show with Jon Stewart," which she watches avidly, and she is also a devoted fan of "Jeopardy." Her favorite band is the Grateful Dead, and she enjoys doing the *New York Times* crossword puzzle. Although she hates to shop (her husband chooses her clothes), she is recognized as a stylish dresser and is fond of Armani suits.

HONORS AND AWARDS

Distinguished Citizens Award (Commonwealth Club of California): 2002

Millard E. Tydings Award for Courage and Leadership in American Politics (University of Maryland's Center for American Politics and Citizenship): 2003

Cesar Chavez Legacy Award (Cesar E. Chavez Foundation): 2003

Alan Cranston Peace Award (The Global Security Institute): 2003

"Unsung Hero" Award (The American Legion): 2004

Community Service Award (The University of California, San Francisco): 2005

Congressional Leadership Award (Minority Business RoundTable): 2006

Excellence in Leadership Award (The Mexican American Legal Defense and Educational Fund): 2007

Peace Award (The American Ireland Fund): 2007

FURTHER READING

Books

Encyclopedia of World Biography Supplement, 2005
Marcovitz, Hal. *Nancy Pelosi*, 2004

Periodicals

Baltimore Sun, Nov. 14, 2002, p.A1
Boston Globe, Feb. 5, 2003, p.D1
Christian Century, Feb. 6, 2007, p.8
Economist, Feb. 24, 2007, p.42
Los Angeles Times, Jan. 4, 2007, p.A1; Jan. 5, 2007, p.A11; Jan. 11, 2007, p.A10; Feb. 9, 2007, p.A14; Mar. 16, 2007, p.A1
Los Angeles Times Magazine, Jan. 26, 2003, p.12
National Catholic Reporter, Jan. 24, 2003, p.3
New Scientist, Jan. 6, 2007, p.8
Newsweek, Nov. 20, 2006, p.50
O, The Oprah Magazine, Apr. 2004, p.66
People, Dec. 2, 2002, p.217
Time, Nov. 20, 2006, p.40; Nov. 27, 2006, p.30
Washington Post, Nov. 19, 2002, p.A25; Nov. 10, 2006, p.C1

Online Articles

http://abcnews.go.com
  (*ABC News*, "Pelosi Conveys Israeli Peace Message to Syria," Apr. 4, 2007)
http://www.cbsnews.com
  (*CBS News*, "Nancy Pelosi: Two Heartbeats Away," Oct. 22, 2006; "Pelosi: No Blank Check for Bush In Iraq," Jan. 7, 2007)
http://www.cnn.com
  (*CNN*, "Pelosi Becomes First Woman House Speaker," Jan. 5, 2007)
http://www.nytimes.com
  (*New York Times*, "A Shift in Power, Starting with 'Madam Speaker,'" Jan. 24, 2007)
http://www.trinitydc.edu/admissions/profile_pelosi.php
  (Trinity University, "Making History, Making Progress," undated)
http://usatoday.com
  (*USA Today*, "Pelosi To Be the First Woman to Lead Congress," Nov. 9, 2006)
http://www.washingtonpost.com
  (Washington Post, "Democrats Won't Try To Impeach President," May 12, 2006)

Online Databases

Biography Resource Center Online, 2007, article from *Encyclopedia of World Biography Supplement*, 2005

ADDRESS

Nancy Pelosi
Office of the Speaker
H-232, US Capitol
Washington, DC 20515

WORLD WIDE WEB SITES

http://www.house.gov/pelosi
http://www.speaker.gov

UPDATE
Jack Prelutsky 1940-
American Children's Poet
First U.S. Children's Poet Laureate

[Editor's Note: Jack Prelutsky was originally featured in *Biography Today Authors,* Vol. 2. In honor of his selection by the Poetry Foundation as the first Children's Poet Laureate, the entry has been expanded and updated to include his most recent accomplishments.]

BIRTH

Jack Prelutsky was born on September 8, 1940, in Brooklyn, New York, to Charles and Dorothea Prelutsky. Charles was an electrician and Dorothea was a homemaker.

YOUTH

While still a baby, Prelutsky was saved from a fire at his family's apartment building in Brooklyn. He was pulled from the flames by his Uncle Charlie, a stand-up comic who played the Borscht Belt (a predominantly Jewish resort area in New York State). Prelutsky has credited his uncle with giving him an appreciation of language as well. "He used to tell me these stupid jokes," Prelutsky remembered, "but they really made me realize what language was about."

Prelutsky grew up in a tough neighborhood in the Bronx, a borough of New York City. "It consisted mainly of Jewish, Irish, and Italian families," he explained. "My father, mother, younger brother and I lived in an apartment house where everyone knew everyone else, just like in a small town. The older people sat on milk crates on the sidewalk and socialized, while the kids played stickball and other street games." The family was poor and Prelutsky never owned a bicycle while growing up. He was often targeted by tougher boys. "I was a sensitive kid in a working-class neighborhood. I got beat up a lot. I was a skinny kid with a big mouth. A bad combination."

"I was an imaginative kid and I would dream of having pets like unicorns and tiny elephants. One of my dreams was that I had my own dragon . . . a small one, of course, that I could manage and train."

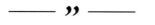

Although he loved animals, Prelutsky could not have any pets in the house because his mother suffered from asthma. So he dreamed of animals he could have for his own. "I was an imaginative kid and I would dream of having pets like unicorns and tiny elephants. One of my dreams was that I had my own dragon . . . a small one, of course, that I could manage and train."

EARLY MEMORIES

"I remembered that my mother used to threaten me with the bogeyman when I would misbehave," Prelutsky once wrote. "My mother would say, 'Wash your hands,' and I would say, 'No.' My mother would say it again and I would say 'No.' She'd say, 'You're making me mad at you,' and I would say, 'I don't care,' and she would say, 'Wash your hands or the bogeyman will get you.' So I washed my hands."

*Prelutsky spends a lot of time with his readers,
as in this visit to a children's bookstore in Seattle.*

EDUCATION

Prelutsky attended the local public schools in the Bronx and hated it. He was bored in class. Although he enjoyed playing word games like Hangman, doing crossword puzzles, and inventing puns, he did not like poetry. "Sometime in elementary school I had a teacher who, in retrospect, did not like poetry herself. She was determined to inflict her views on her captives. The syllabus told her she had to recite a poem once a week. She would pick a boring poem from a boring book and read it in a boring voice, looking bored while she was doing it."

When Prelutsky was in his early teens, his teachers discovered that he had musical talent and suggested that he attend a special high school for the arts. At the High School of Music and Art, he was finally happy. He had a beautiful singing voice and began to take part in high school musical performances. After graduating in 1958, he attended Hunter College for two years. He studied "philosophy, psychology, and a couple of other things," Prelutsky remembered. He flunked English three times before dropping out.

BECOMING A WRITER

Prelutsky had many different jobs before becoming a professional writer. He drove a cab, moved furniture, and worked as a busboy, a potter, a woodworker, and a door-to-door salesman. By the late 1960s, he was working in a bookstore in the Greenwich Village neighborhood in New York City and singing in coffeehouses in his spare time. While working as a singer, he met Bob Dylan. They became friends and admired each other. In fact, Dylan once said that Prelutsky sounded "like a cross between Woody Guthrie and Enrico Caruso."

———— " ————

"Little by little, I got to visiting with children and found out what they liked and didn't like," he recalled. "And I tried to write about the things I wish I had heard about when I was a kid: sibling rivalry, food fights, monsters, dragons, and all that good stuff."

———— " ————

Prelutsky also liked to draw, creating ink drawings of imaginary animals. A friend encouraged him to take his drawings to a New York publishing house. At the last minute, he wrote poems to go with the drawings. Susan Hirshman, the editor, liked his work. He remembered that she said, "You have talent. You should be published." "You like my drawings?" he asked. "Are you kidding?" she said. So the drawings that had taken Prelutsky six months to do were rejected, but the poems he had written in two hours were accepted. He was just 24 at the time. The poems appeared in 1967 in his first book, *A Gopher in the Garden and Other Animal Poems*. "The editor told me I was a natural poet," Prelutsky recalls, "and encouraged me greatly to keep writing. She published my first book, and remained my editor for 37 years, until she retired."

CAREER HIGHLIGHTS

Since that time, Prelutsky has become one of the nation's most beloved poets for young readers. Over a career spanning some four decades, he has sold over a million copies of his books. One of the reasons he has become so popular is because he writes about topics that inspire and fascinate children. Homework, bad meatloaf, and bullies are just some of the topics he has tackled. "Children are flesh and blood. They're just like us, only smaller," he explained. "I write about the things kids care about." In fact, he writes the kinds of poems he would have wanted to read as a kid. Traditional children's

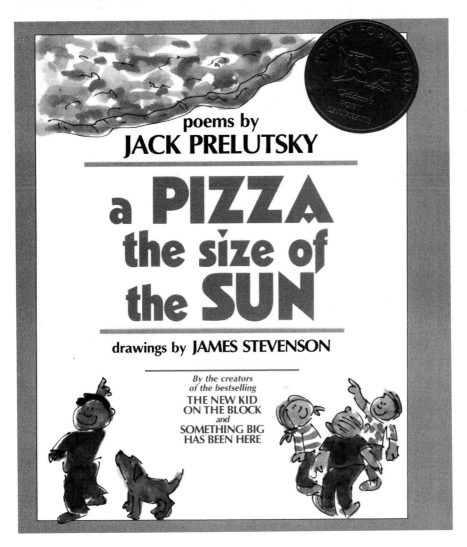

One of Prelutsky's many books of silly poems.

poetry, he once said, is full of "hills and daffodils." But when he was a kid, "we didn't care about that. If I wanted to hear poems, and I wasn't sure I did, I wanted them to be about the cop on the corner, the butcher, the guys in the neighborhood, food fights, dinosaurs, monsters, outer space."

Prelutsky has spent a lot of time with his readers over the years. "Little by little, I got to visiting with children and found out what they liked and didn't like," he recalled. "And I tried to write about the things I wish I had heard

129

about when I was a kid: sibling rivalry, food fights, monsters, dragons, and all that good stuff." He regularly visits schools, libraries, and bookstores where he often sings his poetry to kids, accompanying himself on guitar.

Prelutsky gets ideas for his poems everywhere: from his readers, from his daily life, and from experiences in his past. "Sometimes I take things from my childhood," he said. "My mother was not a particularly good cook. She was a lovely person, but I have never eaten such bad meat loaf." From this experience came the poem "My Mother Made a Meat Loaf," where the meat loaf is so tough it cannot be cut with a cleaver or a drill and must finally be used as bricks to build houses. This type of humor is a large part of what has made his poetry so popular with kids.

> "Writing humorous verse is hard work," Prelutsky has admitted. "For the humor to succeed, every part of the poem must be just right: It requires delicacy. If the poet uses too heavy a hand, the poem goes beyond being funny and turns into something disquieting or even grotesque."

Prelutsky uses language that is full of word play, puns, and all around fun words. His simple and direct language is influenced by the lyrics of folk music. "In folk music, the words are written the way people actually talk, and the melodies are simple and accessible," he says. In choosing his word, Prelutsky explains that he "never talks down" to his readers. "If a $50 word works better than five $10 words, I use the $50 word. I do use words like 'mucilaginous' and 'gelatinous' because children love those words and will find out what they mean."

Silly Poems

Many of Prelutsky's favorite poems are on the silly side. *The Queen of Eene* features poems about people who eat such odd things as cars and basketballs. In *The Sheriff of Rottenshot*, one poem tells of a catfish that is trying to find a mousefish to chase. *A Pizza the Size of the Sun: Poems* contains silly poems about a boy who hides his camel by using "camel-flage," and another one about a salesman with strange goods: "Eyeballs for sale! / Fresh eyeballs for sale! / Delicious, nutritious, / not moldy or stale." *Scranimals* is about an island with unusual creatures that are half-vegetable and half-animal. Among the creatures are the hippopotamushroom, antelopetunia, and

The
Headless Horseman
Rides Tonight

MORE POEMS TO TROUBLE YOUR SLEEP

BY JACK PRELUTSKY
ILLUSTRATED BY ARNOLD LOBEL

One of Prelutsky's most acclaimed books of scary poems.

bananaconda. *Behold the Bold Umbrellaphant and Other Poems* carries the idea even farther, introducing the alarmadillo, the ballpoint penguin, and the clocktopus.

131

"Writing humorous verse is hard work," Prelutsky has admitted. "For the humor to succeed, every part of the poem must be just right: It requires delicacy. If the poet uses too heavy a hand, the poem goes beyond being funny and turns into something disquieting or even grotesque. Conversely, if the poet doesn't push the idea far enough, the incongruities that are supposed to make the poem funny bypass the reader."

Scary Poems

Some of Prelutsky's poems are considered so scary that they have been restricted by librarians, especially those from *Nightmares: Poems to Trouble Your Sleep*. That book was even banned in the school district where he lived. "I believe certain things are inappropriate for children," he allowed. "But I don't believe in shielding children from reality." But Prelutsky's scary poems often provide both chills and chuckles. Many of the poems feature characters from horror stories but in a humorous way. One poem tells of a barber who caters to werewolves; another poem is about a giant's dentist. Despite some librarians' qualms about its subject matter, *Nightmares: Poems to Trouble Your Sleep* was named Best of the Best Books by the *School Library Journal*.

More of Prelutsky's spooky verse appears in *The Headless Horseman Rides Tonight: More Poems to Trouble Your Sleep* and *The Gargoyle on the Roof*. The poems often warn the reader of dangerous creatures: A bogeyman will "crumple your bones" or a ghoul might eat you like he has eaten other children. But many of these poems are chilling in a comical way. One poem from *The Gargoyle on the Roof* is about a vampire grooming himself: "When I look into the mirror / My reflection's never there. / So I always stare at nothing / As I shave and comb my hair." *The Headless Horseman Rides Tonight* was named a *New York Times* Outstanding Book and a *School Library Journal* Best Book.

Earning Acclaim from Readers and Others

Every week, Prelutsky receives about 100 letters from kids who have enjoyed his books. He replies to them in verse: "Thank you for your letter, I'm delighted that you wrote, And very glad to answer you by sending you this note." "I have a talent: I can make anything rhyme," Prelutsky maintained. "The trick was to take the thing I do and work at it—become not just adept, but professional. Just because you can make things rhyme doesn't mean you have anything to say."

Despite the deluge of fan mail, Prelutsky seems to be modest about his talents. "Real poets kind of look down on me," he once said, "though I don't care." But others would disagree. His work has been widely admired by readers, reviewers, and other poets, as in this comment from poet Karen Glenn. "He knows how to have fun and makes boatloads of puns, but Prelutsky is more than a tall, clever child. He is a real poet who knows as much about form, rhythm, and rhyme as he does about burned meatloaf, umbrellaphants, and preposterpusses. He also knows about feelings and, for lack of a better word, soul. . . . He writes real poetry, both formal and informal. He's got rhythm. He's got rhyme. He's even got onomatopoeia, as curious creatures 'honk and quack and squawk.' This is not pretend poetry, gutted of its elements. It's the real thing, filled with alliteration and music. . . . He knows all about form. He writes rhyming couplets. He follows strict rhyme schemes. He writes sonnets—not that kids would ever know it! His poetry is not like spinach, but like chocolate cream pie."

Indeed, Prelutsky's poetic skill is so celebrated that in 1997 he was asked to finish a manuscript that Dr. Seuss had left incomplete when died in 1991. It was an honor to be selected to work on Dr. Seuss's material. Prelutsky finished the story, working with illustrator Lane Smith, and *Hooray for Diffendoofer Day!* was published in 1998. It is the story of a special school where individuality and creative thinking are celebrated.

In 2006, Prelutsky was named the first Children's Poet Laureate by the Poetry Foundation. The laureateship lasts for two years, during which time he will give two major poetry readings and serve as an advisor to the Poetry Foundation on children's literature. The award also includes a $25,000 prize, some of which Prelutsky has said he plans to spend on writing contests for children. According to John Barr, the president of the foundation, "Generations of children have learned to love poetry through Jack Prelutsky's work. His extraordinary service to an important branch of literature makes him the perfect first recipient of the Children's Poet Laureate Award."

Prelutsky heard the news about winning the award while riding on a ferry boat in Seattle. He began jumping up and down and yelling. "I think they thought I was a security risk," he recalled. "I was just shocked and floored. I've never won anything in my life except a two-pound Polish ham in a Vivaldi radio contest, and that was more than 30 years ago."

MAJOR INFLUENCES

Prelutsky has listed Woody Allen, Groucho Marx, and Jimmy Durante as early influences on his work. He also called Dr. Seuss a "genius" and nonsense poet Ogden Nash "my poetic daddy."

MARRIAGE AND FAMILY

Prelutsky married his wife, Carolynn, in 1979. He was on a book tour in Albuquerque, New Mexico. She was a children's librarian with the job of showing him around town. He claims it was love at first sight, and he asked her to marry him the day they met. Just as impetuous as Jack, Carolynn accepted. The couple has lived in Arizona, Boston, New York, and Olympia, Washington. They currently have a loft apartment in downtown Seattle and an apartment on nearby Bainbridge Island. They have no children.

HOBBIES AND OTHER INTERESTS

"I enjoy photography, carpentry, and creating games, collages, and 'found object' sculpture," Prelutsky explained. "Lately I've been teaching myself to draw on the computer." He is also an avid collector of children's books, owning over 4,000 titles. He also collects toy frogs.

SELECTED WRITINGS

A Gopher in the Garden and Other Animal Poems, 1967
The Terrible Tiger, 1970
Toucans and Other Poems, 1970
Nightmares: Poems to Trouble Your Sleep, 1976
It's Halloween, 1977
The Mean Old Hyena, 1978
The Queen of Eene, 1978
The Headless Horseman Rides Tonight: More Poems to Trouble Your Sleep, 1980
Rolling Harvey Down the Hill, 1980
It's Christmas, 1981
The Sheriff of Rottenshot, 1982
Kermit's Garden of Verses, 1982
The Baby Uggs Are Hatching, 1982
It's Thanksgiving, 1982
Zoo Doings: Animal Poems, 1983
It's Valentine's Day, 1983
It's Snowing, It's Snowing!, 1984
The New Kid on the Block, 1984
Ride a Purple Pelican, 1984
Tyrannosaurus Was a Beast, 1988
Something Big Has Been Here, 1990
A. Nonny Mouse Writes Again, 1993
The Dragons Are Singing Tonight, 1993
Monday's Troll, 1996
A Pizza the Size of the Sun: Poems, 1996

The Beauty of the Beast: Poems, 1997
Hooray for Diffendoofer Day!, 1998 (with Dr. Suess)
Dog Days: Rhymes around the Year, 1999
The Gargoyle on the Roof, 1999
The 20th Century Children's Poetry Treasury, 1999
Awful Ogre's Awful Day, 2000
It's Raining Pigs and Noodles: Poems, 2000
The Frogs Wore Red Suspenders: Rhymes, 2002
Scranimals, 2002
If Not for the Cat, 2004
Behold the Bold Umbrellaphant and Other Poems, 2006
Good Sports: Rhymes about Running, Jumping, Throwing, and More, 2007
Me I Am!, 2007

SELECTED HONORS AND AWARDS

Best of the Best Books (*School Library Journal*): 1979, for *Nightmares: Poems to Trouble Your Sleep*
Outstanding Books (*New York Times*): 1980, for *The Headless Horseman Rides Tonight*
Best Books (*School Library Journal*): 1980, for *The Headless Horseman Rides Tonight*; 1981, for *The Wild Baby*; 1983, for *The Random House Book of Poetry for Children*; 1986, for *Read-Aloud Rhymes for the Very Young*
Children's Book of the Year (Child Study Association): 1983, for *The Random House Book of Poetry for Children*
Book of the Year (Library of Congress): 1983, for *The Random House Book of Poetry for Children*
Parents' Choice Award: 1986, for *The New Kid on the Block*
Notable Book (Association for Library Services to Children): 1990, for *Something Big Has Been Here*
Editor's Choice (*Booklist*): 1990, for *Something Big Has Been Here*
Teachers' Choice Award (International Reading Association): 1998, for *The Beauty of the Beast*
Best Book for Young Adults (American Library Association): 1998, for *The Beauty of the Beast*
National Parenting Publication Award: 2001, for *Awful Ogre's Awful Day*
Children's Poet Laureate Award (Poetry Foundation): 2006

FURTHER READING

Books

Contemporary Authors New Revision Series, Vol. 38, 1993
Major Authors and Illustrators for Children and Young Adults, 2002

Something about the Author, Vol. 66, 1991
St. James Guide to Children's Writers, 1999

Periodicals

Allentown (PA) Morning Call, Oct. 4, 1999, p.D1
Chicago Sun-Times, Sep. 28, 2006, p.46
Chicago Tribune, Sep. 28, 2006, p.9
Columbus Dispatch, Jan. 28, 1993, p.B7
Instructor, Sep. 1993, p.81
Publisher's Weekly, Sep. 20, 1991, p.46
San Francisco Chronicle, Feb. 24, 1991, Sunday Review Section, p.10
School Library Journal, Nov. 2006, p. 7
Seattle Post-Intelligencer, Oct. 11, 1990, p.D3; Sep. 28, 2006, p.C1
The Writer, Nov. 1990, p.7

Online Articles

http://www.wildewritingworks.com/int/prelutskyjack.htm
    (*BookPage,* "Interview with Jack Prelutsky," 1993)
http://www.harpercollins.com/authors/13328/Jack_Prelutsky/index.aspx
    (*HarperCollins,* "Author Interview: Jack Prelutsky on *It's Raining Pigs and
    Noodles,*" undated)
http://www.poetryfoundation.org
    (*Poetry Foundation,* "Foundation: Announcements," Sep. 2006)
http://www.poetryfoundation.org/features/feature.children.html?id=178694
    (*Poetry Foundation,* "Never Poke Your Uncle with a Fork: Jack Prelutsky,
    the Nation's First Children's Poet Laureate," undated)

Online Databases

Biography Resource Center Online, 2006, articles from *Contemporary Authors
    Online,* 2006, *Major Authors and Illustrators for Children and Young Adults,*
    2002, and *St. James Guide to Children's Writers,* 1999
Wilson Web, 2006, article from *Fifth Book of Junior Authors and Illustrators:
    Junior Authors Electronic,* 1999

ADDRESS

Jack Prelutsky
Greenwillow Books / HarperCollins
10 East 53rd Street
New York, NY 10022

WORLD WIDE WEB SITES

http://www.jackprelutsky.com
http://www.poetryfoundation.org

Sabriye Tenberken 1970-

German Tibetologist
Founder of the First Tibetan School for the Blind

BIRTH

Sabriye Tenberken was born in 1970 near Bonn, Germany. Her father was a pianist and her mother was a director of a children's theatre. Her mother gave her the name "Sabriye," which means "patience" in Turkish.

YOUTH

Tenberken was born with a degenerative disease of the retina, part of the eye. She began losing her sight at the age of two.

For several years she was able to make out colors and faces, but at the age of 12, she became totally blind. Because other children often teased and taunted her, Tenberken worked hard to make it seem that she was not blind at all. She would even get on the wrong bus to avoid asking the driver where the bus was heading. "Not until I accepted my blindness did I begin to live," she has said.

Tenberken's parents sent her to the Marburg Gymnasium for the Blind and Visually Impaired in Marburg, Germany. There she learned different ways to cope with her blindness, like how to use a white cane and how to read Braille. Braille is a form of written language that uses raised dots on a page to create words. Blind people can "read" the words by running their fingertips across the page. But the school taught the students more than coping skills; it also taught them how to have fun, and Tenberken learned how to ride horses, go kayaking, and ski. "That school infused in me all the confidence I could possibly have," she recounted. She read her first book at the school and made friends there. "I had friends. I was equal and happy."

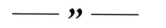

> "All of a sudden, for the first time, I discovered I was not alone," Tenberken said about attending a school for the blind. "Teachers as well as students took me seriously for the first time, treating me on equal footing. The friends I quickly made didn't think I was odd. It was the beginning of a new, wonderful life for me."

Years later, Tenberken described how she felt about her early schooling in her memoir, *My Path Leads to Tibet: The Inspiring Story of How One Young Blind Woman Brought Hope to the Blind Children of Tibet*. "When I was very young, my parents discovered I had some eyesight problems. And yet they decided to send me to school like all the other children. This so-called integrated education wasn't ideal, but it was nonetheless very important to me. It enabled me to know the universe of those who can see normally. But all along I felt distinctly different, and I never understood why. Wherever I went, I received privileged treatment. And I noted that some of the teachers addressed themselves to me in a little voice, as if I was helpless. . . . When I turned 12, I went to a special school for the blind in Marburg. That was a revelation. All of a sudden, for the first time, I discovered I was not alone. It was a great comfort when all the other blind students shared their personal experiences. Teachers as well as students took me seriously for the first

*Tenberken traveled through Tibet on horseback in order to evaluate
the needs of the country's blind population. Here, she is shown riding Romeo
through the fields near her farm in Pelshong near Shigatse.*

time, treating me on equal footing. The friends I quickly made didn't think I
was odd. It was the beginning of a new, wonderful life for me."

Learning about Tibet

Tenberken credits the Marburg school with inspiring her to study Tibetan
culture. While she was in the eighth grade, her class took a field trip to visit
an exhibit on Tibet. The students were allowed to touch religious artifacts,
weapons, and sculptures. They were given a lecture on Tibet's history and
culture. From then on, she wanted to learn more about this Asian country.

Tibet used to be an independent country, but now the Tibet Autonomous
Region is part of China. It is bordered to the north by China and to the
south by India, Nepal, and Bhutan. Tibet is very mountainous and remote, containing the Himalayas and other mountain ranges and many of
the world's highest peaks, including Mount Everest. Political control of
the region has varied: at some points it was independent, and at other
points it was ruled by China. As an independent state, it was a theocracy
ruled by Tibetan monks and led by the Dalai Lama, the spiritual leader of
Tibetan Buddhism.

In the mid-1950s, Tibet and China signed a treaty under which the Dalai
Lama controlled domestic affairs but China controlled foreign and military

affairs. But many Tibetans rebelled against Chinese oppression. In 1959, the Dalai Lama (Tenzin Gyatso) fled to India and began a life in exile. From there, he has advocated Tibetan independence and led non-violent opposition to Chinese rule. Since that time, Tibet has remained an autonomous region of China, and the Dalai Lama has continued the struggle for independence, winning the Nobel Peace Prize in 1989. (For more information on the Dalai Lama, see *Biography Today*, Sep. 1998.)

EDUCATION

After graduating from the Marburg Gymnasium for the Blind and Visually Impaired, Tenberken attended the University of Bonn. There, she was determined to study for a degree in Central Asian Studies, focusing on Tibet. In addition to Mongolian and modern Chinese, she studied modern and classical Tibetan, sociology, and philosophy. She was the first blind person to study Tibetan at the school. But her professors tried to discourage her. The Tibetan language is difficult, and no Braille version existed. But Tenberken was not discouraged. Because there was no Braille version of the Tibetan language, she created one. She also created a Tibetan-German dictionary and, through a computer program she devised, created a way for Tibetan texts to be automatically printed in Braille.

One of her professors offered to take the Braille version to Tibetan authorities, suggesting that they might want Tenberken to visit the country herself and teach it. "It had long been a dream of mine to go to Tibet and make a mark for myself," she recounted. "I couldn't imagine anything more worthwhile than introducing and teaching my reading/writing method to the blind of Tibet!" But the Tibetan authorities were not interested. They did not believe that a blind woman could succeed in such a project. Tenberken earned her degree in Tibetology from the University of Bonn and set out on her plan to visit Tibet.

CHOOSING A CAREER

In May 1997, after finishing college, Tenberken flew to Beijing, China, to meet with Chinese authorities about using her Braille version of Tibetan. She was told by the China Disabled Persons' Federation that Tibet was not a high priority for them. No care for the blind was planned for another ten years. She was even told that blindness was rare in Tibet. Frustrated, she flew to the city of Lhasa, Tibet, to discover the situation for herself. She met a Tibetan paramedic who told her that blindness was common in the country. Poor diet, widespread vitamin A deficiency, and strong ultraviolet rays because of the country's high alti-

These Tibetan children, shown in front of the Potala Palace in Lhasa, Tibet, are students in the school run by Braille without Borders.

tude were the main causes. Tenberken also found that Tibetan society had a strong prejudice against blind people. Many people believed that blindness is a divine punishment for wrong-doing in a previous life or is caused by demons. No charity or medical care organization in Tibet cared for the blind.

Along with two female friends, Tenberken traveled by horseback through-out Tibet to evaluate the needs of the country's blind. Visiting small villages and remote farms, she found many cases where blind children were kept locked indoors for their own safety or because the families were embar-rassed by their condition. Other blind children were begging in the streets. When Tibetans were told that Tenberken was blind, they refused at first to believe it. She could ride a horse, and she knew how to read and write. Her idea to create a school for the blind gave many parents hope that their own children might become successful as well.

When Tenberken returned to Lhasa, a local orphanage offered her space to set up a school for the blind. She returned to Germany and, within six months, raised enough money to finance the project. She and her partner Paul Kronenberg founded Braille Without Borders, a group devoted to bringing education to the blind children of Tibet.

CAREER HIGHLIGHTS

Founding the School

In mid-1998 Tenberken opened the Rehabilitation and Training Center for the Blind in Lhasa, Tibet. The school teaches blind children how to read Braille in Chinese, Tibetan, and English. It also teaches them how to type on a Braille typewriter, how to use a cane to walk, how to cook food, and basic hygiene. There is no charge for the classes or the housing and food the children receive. At any one time, some 30 children between the ages of four and 21 are housed and taught at the school. Many of the teachers are blind children who have already learned Braille. Braille Without Borders prints many books in Braille for use by the children.

Students who finish the program are given the choice to attend regular school with sighted children or return to their home villages. For older students, a course in medical massage therapy is also offered.

The project has endured some major hardships. The school had to move from its original location when Tenberken's partner Paul Kronenberg discovered that school funds were being stolen by the director of the orphanage. Later that winter, Kronenberg almost died when he contracted a severe case of pneumonia. And money ran so short that Tenberken was obliged to put all of her own savings into the school to keep it going. "In the beginning it was horrible," she admitted. "But the obstacles made us stronger. People tried to put limits on me, but limits always show opportunities. I persisted because I *believed* it was possible."

> ——— " ———
>
> *"In the beginning it was horrible," Tenberken said about the early days of Braille Without Borders. "But the obstacles made us stronger. People tried to put limits on me, but limits always show opportunities. I persisted because I* believed *it was possible."*
>
> ——— " ———

The school's annual budget is quite low, only $26,000 a year. Yet, while the Chinese and Tibetan governments now provide some financing for the school, Tenberken and Kronenberg must still spend three months each year in Europe on a fund-raising tour. "The main reason people don't give us money," she explained, "is that we don't raise funds with pity. We don't say, 'Pity our poor blind kids.' People find happy, capable children here. But *happy* doesn't really sell."

Tenberken, Kronenberg, and six blind students achieved an amazing climb of a 23,000-foot Tibetan mountain, which was filmed for the documentary Blindsight. *In this still from the movie, Tenberken is shown on a training hike prior to the ascent.*

In 2004 Tenberken and Kronenberg opened a training farm for blind adults in Shigatse, Tibet. Here older blind persons are taught basic farm skills so that they can operate a dairy farm. They learn to feed and care for the animals, plant and harvest crops for food, milk cows, and even make cheese. The farm hopes to sell the cheese it produces throughout China in the near future.

Blindsight

Also in 2004, Tenberken had the opportunity for an incredible adventure. She, Kronenberg, and six teenaged students from their school undertook a three-week climb of Lhakpa Ri, a 23,000-foot mountain in Tibet near Mount Everest. The trip was led by Erik Weihenmayer, a professional mountain climber who is also the first blind man to have climbed Mount Everest. On the expedition, they made use of a number of tools Weihenmayer had invented specifically to help blind people climb safely. Their impressive ascent was recorded by documentary filmmaker Lucy Walker.

The resulting feature was released in 2006 as *Blindsight*. Nominated for several international awards, it won the Audience Award for Best Documentary Film at several notable film festivals, including the 2006 AFI Film Festival, the 2007 Berlin Film Festival, and the Palm Springs Film Festival. In addition, Tenberken wrote a book about the experience, *Das siebte Jahr: Von Tibet nach Indien* (The Seventh Year: From Tibet to India), which is available only in German. In it, she chronicles the climb and profiles the students who undertook the adventure.

Recent Projects

While her work in Tibet continues, Tenberken has not stopped there. In 2006 Braille Without Borders began construction of the International Centre for Development and Project Planning (ICDeP) in Kerala, India. The need for the new school is clear when viewing statistics from the World Health Organization, cited on the Braille Without Borders web site. Worldwide, 161 million people live with a disabling visual impairment, including 37 million people who are blind and 124 million people with low vision. About 80% live in developing countries.

The new center will teach blind people from all over the developing world how to set up and manage a school for the blind in their own countries. Students will study management, fundraising, public relations, project planning, computer technology, English and communication skills, and other skills necessary to running an organization. The training will enable the students to set up and lead social projects in their own communities. With this new project, Tenberken hopes to educate and empower many more blind people around the world.

HOME AND FAMILY

Tenberken, who is not married, lives with her partner, Paul Kronenberg. He is Dutch and has worked as a designer and construction coordinator for the Swiss Red Cross and for other organizations. He supervises all construction projects for Braille Without Borders and teaches people bookkeeping and computer skills to run the organization's office.

WRITINGS

My Path Leads to Tibet: The Inspiring Story of How One Young Blind Woman Brought Hope to the Blind Children of Tibet, 2003

HONORS AND AWARDS

Norgall Prize (International Women's Club): 2000
Charity Bambi (Burda, Germany): 2000
Zilveren Jandaia (Stichting kerk en Wereld, Holland): 2001
Global Leader of Tomorrow (World Economic Forum): 2001
Albert Schweizer Award (Wolfgang von Goethe Association): 2002
Knight (Order of Oranje Nassau, Netherlands): 2003
XX Factor All Star (*Outside Magazine*): 2003
Christopher Award: 2004, for *My Path Leads to Tibet*
Asian Hero Award (*Time* magazine): 2004
European Hero Award (*Time* magazine): 2004
Leile Luce Hadley Award (World Wings Trust): 2005
Bundesverdienst kreuz (government of Germany): 2005
Chomolongma Friendship Award (government of the Tibet Autonomous Region): 2006
National Friendship Award (government of China): 2006
Mother Teresa Award: 2006

FURTHER READING

Books

Contemporary Authors, Vol. 234, 2005
Tenberken, Sabriye. *My Path Leads to Tibet: The Inspiring Story of How One Young Blind Woman Brought Hope to the Blind Children of Tibet*, 2003

Periodicals

Kirkus Reviews, Nov. 1, 2002, p.1603
New York Times, Sep. 20, 2003, p.A4
O, The Oprah Magazine, Aug. 2005, p. 222
Publishers Weekly, Nov. 11, 2002, p.48
School Library Journal, May, 2003, p.181

Online Articles

http://www.climbingblind.org
    (*Climbing Blind Tibet Expedition 2004*, "Team Profiles," undated)
http://www.oprah.com
    (*Oprah.com*, "Phenomenal Females," undated)
http://www.1000peacewomen.org
    (*Peace Women across the Globe*, "Sabriye Tenberken," undated)
http://www.time.com/time/asia
    (*Time Asia*, "Sabriye Tenberken," Oct. 4, 2004)
http://www.time.com/time/europe
    (*Time Europe*, "The Visionary," Oct. 2, 2004)

Online Databases

Biography Resource Center Online, 2007, article from *Contemporary Authors Online*, 2005

ADDRESS

Sabriye Tenberken
Arcade Publishing
116 John Street #2810
New York, NY 10038
Blind Without Borders
E-mail: blztib@t-online.de

WORLD WIDE WEB SITES

http://www.braillewithoutborders.org
http://www.blindsightthemovie.com

Muhammad Yunus 1940-

Bangladeshi Banker and Human Rights Activist
Winner of the 2006 Nobel Peace Prize for His Work
in Fighting Poverty

BIRTH

Muhammad Yunus was born on June 28, 1940, in the village of
Bathua, near the port city of Chittagong. That area was then in
Eastern Bengal, part of British-controlled India, and is now
part of Pakistan. Yunus grew up in the jeweler's section of
town, with the sounds of street vendors, jugglers, and beggars
right outside his house. His father, Muhammad Dula Mia, was
a goldsmith who kept his jewelry shop on the ground floor.

147

His mother, Sofia Khatun, was a major influence on Yunus. "Full of compassion and kindness, Mother always put money away for any poor relatives who visited us from distant villages," he remembered. "It was she, by her concern for the poor and the disadvantaged, who helped me discover my interest in economics and social reform." Yunus was the third of 14 children, although five of his siblings died in infancy.

THE CREATION OF BANGLADESH

The port city of Chittagong is now part of Bangladesh. But at that time, Chittagong was part of India. Beginning in the mid to late 1700s, much of India was ruled by Great Britain. India was primarily Hindu, although there was also a minority Muslim population. In the 1900s, as India fought for its independence, the minority Muslim population began working for an independent Muslim nation. In 1947 India became independent from Great Britain, and the Muslim nation of Pakistan was formed. But the nation of Pakistan was divided into two parts: West Pakistan, along India's western border, and East Pakistan, along India's eastern border. The two parts of Pakistan were separated by 1,600 miles of Indian territory. At this point, when Pakistan was formed, Yunus was seven.

The separation of India and Pakistan was not smooth. Hindus who lived in Pakistan territory and Muslims who lived in Indian territory began a great migration, with some 13 million people on the move. Terrible violence flared up, and many refugees were massacred. War broke out between the two nations over contested regions. In addition, the new nation of Pakistan experienced tremendous political instability. The two parts of the country were divided not only by geography, but also by ethnic and religious issues. Dissension between West and East Pakistan grew into civil war, and in 1971 East Pakistan declared its independence and became the sovereign nation of Bangladesh.

YOUTH

Yunus grew up initially in the village of Bathua before his family moved to the city of Chittagong. There, his father was a successful jeweler, but he had only a seventh grade education. Still, he always valued education and taught his children to do the same. Yunus and his older sister, Salam, loved to read so much that they spent part of every afternoon in the waiting room of the local doctor's office, reading the magazines. He and his sister also enjoyed going to the movies, taking pictures with their camera, and eating out in restaurants. His favorite dish was "potato chop," a roasted potato filled with fried onion and vinegar.

Dealing with Mental Illness

When Yunus was nine, his mother began to act strangely, apparently suffering from mental illness. Mental illness ran in his mother's family—her mother and two sisters had suffered from it—but no doctor was ever able to diagnose or treat it. Yunus wrote about this difficult time in his autobiography, *Banker to the Poor: Micro-Lending and the Battle Against World Poverty*. Here, he described his mother's unpredictable behavior. "Her behavior was increasingly abnormal," he wrote. "In her calmer periods she would talk disjointed nonsense to herself. For hours on end she would sit in prayer, read the same page of a book, or recite a poem over and over without stopping. In her more disturbed periods, she would insult people in a loud voice and use vulgar language. Sometimes she would hurl abuse at a neighbor, a friend, or a family member, but other times she would rant away at politicians or even long-dead figures. Her mind would turn against imaginary enemies and then, without much warning, she would become violent."

The experience was clearly a difficult one for Yunus, who helped his father restrain his mother or protect his siblings from her attacks. His mother gradually lost track of many day-to-day activities, including the children's schoolwork and studies. Still, Yunus demonstrated resilience at an early age. In his autobiography, he recounted how he and his siblings learned to treat their mother's illness with a certain humor. "'What is the weather forecast?' we would ask one another when we tried to predict mother's mood for the next few hours," he recalled. "To avoid provoking a fresh bout of abuse, we gave code names to various persons in the household: Number 2, Number 4, and so on."

"Her behavior was increasingly abnormal," Yunus said about his mother. "In her more disturbed periods, she would insult people in a loud voice and use vulgar language. Sometimes she would hurl abuse at a neighbor, a friend, or a family member. . . . Her mind would turn against imaginary enemies and then, without much warning, she would become violent."

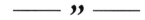

EDUCATION

As a young boy, Yunus attended elementary school, called primary school, first at the local village school in Bathua and then in Chittagong. He later

Yunus with his class in the Graduate Program in Economic Development at Vanderbilt University, 1966. Yunus is in the second row from the bottom, the second from the left.

attended Chittagong Collegiate School, the rough equivalent of high school. While in secondary school, Yunus joined the Boy Scouts, an American-based organization with troops around the world. With the Scouts, he found a role model in assistant headmaster, Quazi Sahib. "I had always been a natural leader," Yunus said, "but Quazi Sahib's moral influence taught me to think high and channel my passions." He traveled to several other countries with the Scouts and attended the World Boy Scouts Jamboree in Canada in 1955. To return home, he traveled across Europe and Asia by road.

Yunus next attended Chittagong College where he enjoyed a wide range of creative interests, including theater, art, photography, and writing. In 1957, he enrolled at Dhaka University in the department of economics. He completed his Bachelor of Arts (BA) degree in 1960 and his Master of Arts (MA) degree in 1961. He then spent several years working in business and also as a lecturer at Chittagong College before returning to school.

In 1965, Yunus earned a Fulbright Scholarship to study in the United States. The Fulbright Program, which is sponsored by the U.S. Department of State, is an international exchange program that enables U.S. students, scholars, and professionals to study abroad, and also enables their counterparts in other countries to study in the U.S. The program is designed to foster international relationships and "to increase mutual understanding between the people of the United States and the people of other countries."

The Fulbright Scholarship allowed Yunus to study development economics at Vanderbilt University in Nashville, Tennessee. In the United States, he was deeply influenced by the student activism and civil rights movement of the 1960s. Martin Luther King Jr. became a personal hero. "When I arrived in the U.S. in the 1960s, it was a real shock, coming from a conservative Muslim family," he said. Yunus completed work on his doctoral degree or doctorate (PhD) in about 1969 or 1970 and then was appointed an instructor at Middle Tennessee State University.

Meanwhile, the movement for independence was taking hold in East Pakistan. Yunus returned home in 1972 to help build the newly independent country of Bangladesh and soon became an economics professor at Chittagong University.

CAREER HIGHLIGHTS

The 1970s, when Yunus was beginning his career as an economic professor, marked a difficult time for Bangladesh. The country was still trying to build an infrastructure after recently becoming independent. Political disorder was ongoing. Then in 1974 floods devastated the grain crop, and a horrible famine gripped the nation. People were literally dying in the streets, collapsing of starvation.

Working as a college professor, Yunus felt frustrated teaching "elegant theories of economics" that did nothing to relieve people's suffering. One day in 1976, he met Sufiya Begum, a 21-year old mother of three who made stools out of bamboo. Because Begum did not have the money to buy her own bamboo, she had to borrow from a trader who sold her finished stools. As a result, she ended up with a profit of only two cents per stool. "Her life was a form of bonded labor, or slavery," Yunus recalled. With the help of one of his students, he discovered that 42 villagers owed a total of less than $27 to traders. "My God. My God," he exclaimed. "All this misery in all these families all for only the lack of $27!" He reached into his pocket and gave his student $27 to distribute directly to the villagers. They could pay him back whenever they had the money. He would not charge interest.

So began Yunus's innovative banking practices. Hailed as the "banker to the poor," he has revolutionized the field of banking by making small loans available to millions of people who had previously been denied credit. Banks traditionally have refused to lend money to the poor because they lack possessions, such as houses or cars, that can be seized if they fail to pay back the loan. Yunus, however, found a new way to guarantee loans, using "borrowing groups" to provide much-needed structure and support.

Developing a Program of Group Support

Yunus called his experimental lending project the Grameen ("Village") Bank program. Wanting to expand his program, he asked the branch manager of a local bank to loan money to the poor villagers of Jobra. The branch manager told him he doubted the bank would want to lend to people who had no possessions to guarantee payment. Yunus believed that people would pay back their loans because they'd recognize credit as a chance to have a better life. Refusing to give up, he contacted a higher level official at the bank's district branch. Although the bank official refused to lend directly to the poor, he agreed to lend money to Yunus for the villagers. Then Yunus lent the money to the villagers. All the borrowers paid back their loans in full and on time, proving the bank officials wrong.

> "Conventional banks look at what has already been acquired by a person," Yunus explained. "Grameen looks at the potential that is waiting to be unleashed in a person. Conventional banks are owned by the rich, generally men. Grameen Bank is owned by poor women."

With this approach, Yunus defied the stereotype of a banker. Many of his lending practices are the exact opposite of those used by conventional banks. "Conventional banks look at what has already been acquired by a person," he explained. "Grameen looks at the potential that is waiting to be unleashed in a person. Conventional banks are owned by the rich, generally men. Grameen Bank is owned by poor women."

From the beginning, Yunus made borrowing groups the centerpiece of his program. "Subtle and not so subtle peer pressure keeps each group member in line with the broader objectives of the credit program," he wrote in his autobiography *Banker to the Poor*. Borrowers come together in five-member groups. Each member must undergo at least seven days of training and pass a test to be approved by the bank. Once the first two people in the group have completed their weekly payments, the third and fourth, and then the fifth, can apply for a loan. Borrowers are required to accumulate savings. Several groups meet together at regional centers, where payments are collected and questions discussed.

Borrowers must also promise to abide by the "Sixteen Decisions." These principles commit members to leading productive and purposeful lives. In his autobiography *Banker to the Poor,* Yunus listed all Sixteen Decisions. The first deci sion, for instance, reads: "We shall follow and advance the four principles of the Grameen Bank—discipline, unity, courage, and hard work—in all walks of our lives." Other decisions involve matters such as living in a healthy manner,

Bangladeshi women Monju Begum (left) and Sahera Khatun (right) feed their chickens, which they bought with money loaned by the Grameen Bank.

keeping family size small, educating children, keeping homes in good repair, and prohibiting child marriage. Some members choose to chant the Sixteen Decisions.

Loaning to Women

Yunus quickly found a difference between women and men: female borrowers used their loans more wisely than male borrowers did. Male borrowers spent the money on themselves, while female borrowers used it to improve the lives of everyone in the family. However, Yunus knew that it wouldn't be easy to lend money to women in a largely Muslim country like Bangladesh. Many women were afraid to be seen by an unfamiliar man like Yunus, and they were even more reluctant to discuss banking matters with him. Women often told him that they couldn't accept loans because their husbands handled the money. Gradually, with the help of female bank workers, Yunus built up a corps of female borrowers. "Once we were able to convince one woman, our work was half done," he explained. "She

Borrowers with the Grameen Bank walk to the bank to pay their loan installments in the village of Basta, near Dhaka.

then was an example that convinced her friends and then her friends' families and so on."

Yunus also faced opposition from resentful husbands and conservative religious leaders. Many husbands, though, became more supportive of their wives' involvement with the bank once their families had enough food to eat. On the religious front, some mullahs (Muslim clerics) preached that Grameen aimed to destroy Islam. Yunus argued back that, in Islamic history, women have long been powerful figures. Nothing in Islam, he said, prevents them from taking loans to lift themselves and their families out of poverty. Over the years, the Grameen Bank's percentage of female borrowers has risen to about 97 percent.

Expanding the Loan Program

Some skeptics doubted that this system of small loans, known as "microcredit," could work outside of Yunus's own region of Bangladesh. One bank manager, for example, attributed the success of the lending program to Yunus's personality. Determined to prove the naysayers wrong, he took a leave of absence from the university and spread his program to five new areas of Bangladesh in 1982. In 1983, he restructured his bank as an independent institution. As an independent bank, Grameen grew quickly, giving rise to centers all over Bangladesh. The Grameen model has spread to some 100 countries around the world, including the United States.

In 1985, Arkansas Governor (and later U.S. President) Bill Clinton became an admirer of Yunus. Governor Clinton persuaded him to help create a new credit program for low-income people in Arkansas. Critics predicted that such a system would fail in the United States because people were accustomed to large, rather than small, loans. However, Yunus's first recruit—a woman seeking $375 to open a beautician business—proved the critics wrong. Arkansas's Good Faith program grew to reach hundreds of low-income people in the state. Later, Yunus brought a similar program to Cherokee women in Oklahoma. During the next two decades, the idea of microcredit continued to spread.

In recent years, Yunus has added new programs to combat poverty. In 2003, he launched a program focusing on beggars. With the help of interest-free loans, about 5,000 individuals have gone from begging to selling small items such as snacks and toys door to door. He also created a mobile phone company, Grameen Phone. Nearly 300,000 "telephone ladies" provide cell phone service by the minute to the villages of Bangladesh. "This is a form of globalization," said Yunus. "They have the whole world at their fingertips." In addition, Grameen has established two new business ventures. The first is a yogurt factory to produce fortified yogurt, and the second is a chain of eye-care hospitals.

By 2006, Grameen Bank had lent $5.72 billion and claimed a 98 percent repayment rate. Yunus had won the praise of numerous celebrities, including the rock star Bono, TV host Oprah Winfrey, and former president Bill Clinton. In addition, he had won support from members on both sides of the political spectrum. Conservatives liked his message of entrepreneurship and self-reliance, while liberals applauded his commitment to large-scale social welfare.

Winning the Nobel Peace Prize

On October 13, 2006, Yunus won the prestigious Nobel Peace Prize. The award was divided into two equal parts: to Muhammad Yunus and to Grameen Bank. In awarding the Nobel Peace Prize to Yunus, the committee acknowledged the link between poverty and world peace. "Lasting peace cannot be achieved unless large population groups find ways in which to break out of poverty," the Norwegian Nobel Committee said in its presentation speech. The committee praised Yunus as "a leader who has managed to translate visions into practical action for the benefit of millions of people, not only in Bangladesh but across cultures and civilizations."

As soon as people in Bangladesh heard the news, they started bringing flowers to Yunus's home in Dhaka, the capital of Bangladesh. His phone kept ringing. "This prize is so overwhelming; it will affect our work tremendously," he told a reporter. "It will bring the issues I'm raising to the attention of people who can make a difference in the world."

Yunus received congratulations from people around the world. Former President Bill Clinton had this to say. "Hillary and I first met Muhammad Yunus when I was Governor, and he inspired us to create a micro-finance program in Arkansas based on his model. Muhammad proved that the poor are credit worthy and that a micro-finance effort can be self-sustainable, create growth and spread peace. . . . Because of his efforts, millions of people, most of them women, have had the chance to improve their lives and we are all better off as a result. . . . The committee could not have selected anyone better." And former United Nations Secretary-General Kofi Annan added these words: "Thanks to Professor Yunus and the Grameen Bank, micro-finance has proved its value as a way for low-income families to break the vicious circle of poverty, for productive enterprises to grow, and for communities to prosper. They have provided a powerful weapon to help the world . . . by helping people change their lives for the better—especially those who need it most."

> **"This year's prize gives highest honor and dignity to the hundreds of millions of women all around the world who struggle every day to make a living and bring hope for a better life for their children,"** Yunus said. **"This is a historic moment for them."**

In his acceptance speech, Yunus emphasized several key points. He called poverty a threat to peace, a potential cause of terrorism, and a denial of human rights. He also said this: "Since the Nobel Peace Prize was announced, I have received endless messages from around the world, but what moves me most are the calls I get almost daily, from the borrowers of Grameen Bank in remote Bangladeshi villages, who just want to say how proud they are to have received this recognition. . . . All borrowers of Grameen Bank are celebrating this day as the greatest day of their lives.

After receiving the Nobel Peace Prize, Yunus poses with the medal and diploma.

They are gathering around the nearest television set in their villages all over Bangladesh, along with other villagers, to watch the proceedings of this ceremony. This year's prize gives highest honor and dignity to the hundreds of millions of women all around the world who struggle every day to make a living and bring hope for a better life for their children. This is a historic moment for them."

Yunus argued that change is possible. "We get what we want, or what we don't refuse. We accept the fact that we will always have poor people around us, and that poverty is part of human destiny. This is precisely why we continue to have poor people around us. If we firmly believe that poverty is unacceptable to us, and that it should not belong to a civilized society, we would have built appropriate institutions and policies to create a poverty-free world. We wanted to go to the moon, so we went there. We achieve what we want to achieve. If we are not achieving something, it is because we have not put our minds to it. We create what we want."

Yunus believes that we can eliminate poverty altogether. He hopes that one day, children will wonder why the world allowed poverty to go on for so long. "I firmly believe that we can create a poverty-free world if we collectively believe in it. In a poverty-free world, the only place you would be able to see poverty is in the poverty museums. When school children take a tour of the poverty museums, they would be horrified to see the misery and indignity that some human beings had to go through. They would blame their forefathers for tolerating this inhuman condition, which existed for so long, for so many people."

MARRIAGE AND FAMILY

In 1970 Yunus was married to a Russian-born American, Vera Forostenko. They had met at Vanderbilt in Tennessee, where both were studying at the time, and then moved to Bangladesh. They had a daughter, Monica, born in 1977. Living in Bangladesh and struggling with the cultural differences, Forostenko felt that the environment was not a good place to raise a child. The couple divorced, and Forostenko moved to New Jersey and raised Monica there.

In 1980 Yunus was married to Afrozi Begum, a physics professor. Begum was a fellow Bangladeshi who had studied in England. She and Yunus had had similar experiences in living both in western and in eastern cultures, which eliminated the issue of cultural differences. They had one daughter, Deena, born in 1986. They live in Dhaka, the capital of Bangladesh.

HOBBIES AND OTHER INTERESTS

What does Nobel Peace Prize winner Muhammad Yunus do for fun? When Vanderbilt University professor James Foster asked this question, Yunus replied that he spends his spare time "thinking of new strategies to help people help themselves." He also spends much of his time speaking to young people. "I'm encouraging young people to become social business entrepreneurs and contribute to the world, rather than just making money," he said. "Making money is no fun. Contributing to and changing the world is a lot more fun." Lauded as an idealist and a visionary, Yunus describes himself as "a stubborn guy." Throughout his career, he has persevered despite numerous obstacles. "If I feel it in my gut that something is the right thing to do, I do not give it up," he said.

WRITINGS

Banker to the Poor: Micro-Lending and the Battle Against World Poverty, 1999
  (with Alan Jolis)

SELECTED HONORS AND AWARDS

President's Award (Bangladesh): 1978
Ramon Magsaysay Award (Philippines): 1984, for community leadership
CARE Humanitarian Award: 1993
World Food Prize: 1994
International Simon Bolivar Prize (Venezuala and UNESCO): 1996
Help for Self-Help Prize (Stromme Foundation, Norway): 1997
Indira Gandhi Prize (Indira Gandhi Memorial Turst, India): 1998, for
  peace, disarmament, and development
King Hussein Humanitarian Leadership Award (King Hussein Foundation, Jordan): 2000
Mahatma Gandhi Award (M.K. Gandhi Institute of Nonviolence): 2002
National Merit Order Award (President of the Republic of Colombia):
  2003
25 Most Influential Business Persons of the Past 25 Years (PBS and Wharton School of Business): 2004
Innovation Award (*The Economist*): 2004, for social and economic innovation
Nobel Peace Prize: 2006, to Muhammad Yunus and Grameen Bank
Greatest Entrepreneurs of All Time (*Business Week*): 2007

FURTHER READING

Books

Contemporary Heroes and Heroines, Book III, 1998
Library of International Biographies—Volume 1: Activists, 1990
Yunus, Muhammad, with Alan Jolis. *Banker to the Poor: Micro-Lending and the Battle Against World Poverty*, 1999

Periodicals

Atlantic Monthly, Dec. 1995, p.40
Current Biography International Yearbook, 2002
Current Events, Nov. 10, 2006, p.1
Los Angeles Times, Jan. 25, 1998, p.M3
People, Oct. 30, 2006, p.120
Time, Oct. 23, 2006, p.21
Washington Post, Apr. 18. 2004, pp.A1 and A25

Online Articles

http://www.businessweek.com
   (*Business Week*, "Can Technology Eliminate Poverty: Grameen Bank
   Founder Muhammad Yunus Thinks So. And He Explains Why Changing
   the World Is a Lot More Fun than Just Making Money," Dec. 26, 2005)
http://www:grameen-info.org
   (*Grameen Bank*, "Is Grameen Bank Different From Conventional
   Banks?" Feb. 2007)
http://www.pbs.org/opb/thenewheroes/meet/yunus.html
   (*PBS*, "Meet the New Heroes: Muhammad Yunus," undated)

Online Databases

Biography Resource Center Online, 2007, articles from *Contemporary Heroes
   and Heroines, Book III*, 1998, and *Library of International Biographies—Volume 1: Activists*, 1990

ADDRESS

Muhammad Yunus
PublicAffairs Books
250 West 57th Street
Suite 1321
New York, NY 10107

Muhammad Yunus
Grameen Bank Bhavan
Mirpur-1, Dhaka-1216
Bangladesh

WORLD WIDE WEB SITES

http://muhammadyunus.org
http://www.grameen-info.org

Photo and Illustration Credits

Front cover photos: Anthony: Doug Pensinger/Getty Images; Carter: Jim Cooper/AP Photo; Ferrera: UGLY BETTY: THE COMPLETE FIRST SEASON - THE BETTIFED VERSION copyright © 2007 Buena Vista Home Entertainment. All Rights Reserved.; Pelosi: U.S. Office of the Speaker (www.speaker.gov).

Carmelo Anthony/Photos: Gary Dineen/NBAE/Getty Images (p. 9); Ida Mae Astute/ABC/ Getty Images (p. 11); Syracuse University Athletic Communications (p. 13); Garrett W. Ellwood/NBAE/Getty Images (p. 17); Chris Carlson/AP Photo (p. 19); Jeffrey Bottari/NBAE/Getty Images (p. 23); Garrett W. Ellwood/NBAE/Getty Images (p. 24).

Regina Carter/Photos: Bill Phelps/copyright © 2007 Universal Music Group (p. 29); Scott Gries/Emigrant Savings Bank/Getty Images (p. 32); Kathy Willens/AP Photo (p. 36); Rick Diamond/WireImage.com (p. 39). CD cover: SOMETHING FOR GRACE copyright © 1997 Atlantic Recording Corporation. Cover design by Elizabeth Barrett. Cover photo by Darryl Turner (p. 35).

Kortney Clemons/Photos: Steve Tessler/courtesy of Pennsylvania State University Athletics (pp. 43, 50); Troy Hopkins/courtesy of Soldiers Magazine, March 2006 (p. 46); Carolyn Kaster/AP Photo (p. 48).

Miley Cyrus/Photos: HANNAH MONTANA: POP STAR PROFILE copyright © 2007 Disney. All Rights Reserved. (pp. 53, 55, 57); CD cover: HANNAH MONTANA 2: MEET MILEY CYRUS copyright © 2007 Universal Music Group (p. 59).

Fall Out Boy/Photos: PRNewsFoto/Virgin Mobile USA, LLC (p. 63); Ken Schles/copyright © 2007 Universal Music Group (p. 65); Scott Gries/Getty Images (p. 73). CD covers: TAKE THIS TO YOUR GRAVE copyright © 2003 Fueled By Ramen Inc. All rights reserved. Cover design by Mike Joyce (stereo-design.com). Cover photo by Ryan Bakerink. (p. 67); FROM UNDER THE CORK TREE copyright © 2007 Universal Music Group (p. 70).

America Ferrera/Photos: Peter Kramer/Getty Images (p. 77); Nicola Goode/REAL WOMEN HAVE CURVES copyright © 2002 HBO (p. 81); Diyah Pera/THE SISTERHOOD OF THE TRAVELING PANTS copyright © 2005 Warner Bros. (p. 83); Bob Long/HFPA/Getty Images (p. 87). UGLY BETTY: THE COMPLETE FIRST SEASON—THE BETTIFED VERSION copyright © 2007 Buena Vista Home Entertainment. All Rights Reserved. (p. 85).

Wendy Kopp/Photos: Jean-Christian Bourcart/courtesy of Teach For America (pp. 93, 95, 98); Elise Amendola/AP Photo (p.102).

Cumulative Names Index

This cumulative index includes the names of all individuals profiled in *Biography Today* since the debut of the series in 1992.

For cumulative general, places of birth, and birthday indexes, please see biographytoday.com.

163

For cumulative general, places of birth, and birthday indexes, please see biographytoday.com.

165

For cumulative general, places of birth, and birthday indexes, please see biographytoday.com.

For cumulative general, places of birth, and birthday indexes, please see biographytoday.com.

169

For cumulative general, places of birth, and birthday indexes, please see biographytoday.com.

171

For cumulative general, places of birth, and birthday indexes, please see biographytoday.com.

For cumulative general, places of birth, and birthday indexes, please see biographytoday.com.

175

For cumulative general, places of birth, and birthday indexes, please see biographytoday.com.

For cumulative general, places of birth, and birthday indexes, please see biographytoday.com.

177

Biography Today

For ages 9 and above

General Series

B iography Today **General Series** includes a unique combination of current biographical profiles that teachers and librarians — and the readers themselves — tell us are most appealing. The **General Series** is available as a 3-issue subscription; hardcover annual cumulation; or subscription plus cumulation.

Within the **General Series**, your readers will find a variety of sketches about:

- Authors
- Musicians
- Political leaders
- Sports figures
- Movie actresses & actors
- Cartoonists
- Scientists
- Astronauts
- TV personalities
- and the movers & shakers in many other fields!

ONE-YEAR SUBSCRIPTION
- 3 softcover issues, 6" x 9"
- Published in January, April, and September
- 1-year subscription, list price $62. **School and library price $60**
- 150 pages per issue
- 10 profiles per issue
- Contact sources for additional information
- Cumulative Names Index

HARDBOUND ANNUAL CUMULATION
- Sturdy 6" x 9" hardbound volume
- Published in December
- List price $69. **School and library price $62 per volume**
- 450 pages per volume
- 30 profiles — includes all profiles found in softcover issues for that calendar year
- Cumulative General Index, Places of Birth Index, and Birthday Index

SUBSCRIPTION AND CUMULATION COMBINATION
- $99 for 3 softcover issues plus the hardbound volume

For Cumulative General, Places of Birth, and Birthday Indexes, please see www.biographytoday.com.

"Biography Today will be useful in elementary and middle school libraries and in public library children's collections where there is a need for biographies of current personalities. High schools serving reluctant readers may also want to consider a subscription."

— *Booklist,* American Library Association

"Highly recommended for the young adult audience. Readers will delight in the accessible, energetic, tell-all style; teachers, librarians, and parents will welcome the clever format [and] intelligent and informative text. It should prove especially useful in motivating 'reluctant' readers or literate nonreaders."

— *MultiCultural Review*

"Written in a friendly, almost chatty tone, the profiles offer quick, objective information. While coverage of current figures makes *Biography Today* a useful reference tool, an appealing format and wide scope make it a fun resource to browse." — *School Library Journal*

"The best source for current information at a level kids can understand."

— Kelly Bryant, School Librarian, Carlton, OR

"Easy for kids to read. We love it! Don't want to be without it."

— Lynn McWhirter, School Librarian, Rockford, IL